# GRAY AREAS

Published by LifeWay Press®
© 2013 Mike Glenn

No part of this work may be reproduced or transmitted in any form or by any means, electronic or mechanical, including photocopying and recording, or by any information storage or retrieval system, except as may be expressly permitted in writing by the publisher. Requests for permission should be addressed in writing to LifeWay Press®, One LifeWay Plaza, Nashville, TN 37234-0152.

ISBN: 978-1-4158-7969-6
Item: 005560881

Dewey Decimal Classification Number: 241
Subject Heading: BELIEF AND DOUBT \ FAITH \ CHRISTIAN ETHICS

Printed in the United States of America.

Young Adult Ministry Publishing
LifeWay Church Resources
One LifeWay Plaza
Nashville, Tennessee 37234-0152

We believe that the Bible has God for its author; salvation for its end; and truth, without any mixture of error, for its matter and that all Scripture is totally true and trustworthy. To review LifeWay's doctrinal guideline, please visit *www.lifeway.com/ doctrinalguideline*.

All Scripture quotations are taken from the Holman Christian Standard Bible®, Copyright © 1999, 2000, 2002, 2003, 2009 by Holman Bible Publishers. Used by permission. Holman Christian Standard Bible®, Holman CSB®, and HCSB® are federally registered trademarks of Holman Bible Publishers.

Cover design by Lauren Randalls Ervin.

# TABLE OF CONTENTS

# WELCOME

## VALUES FOR SMALL GROUPS

Meeting together to study God's Word and experience life together is an exciting adventure. Here are values to consider for small-group experiences:

**COMMUNITY:** God is relational, so He created us to live in relationship with Him and each other. Authentic community involves sharing life together and connecting on many levels with others in our group.

**INTERACTIVE BIBLE STUDY:** God gave the Bible as our instruction manual for life. We need to deepen our understanding of God's Word. People learn and remember more as they wrestle with truth and learn from others. Bible discovery and group interaction will enhance spiritual growth.

**EXPERIENTIAL GROWTH:** Beyond solely reading, studying, and dissecting the Bible, being a disciple of Christ involves marrying knowledge and experience. We do this by taking questions to God, opening a dialogue with our hearts, and utilizing other ways to listen to God speak (other people, nature, circumstances, etc.). Experiential growth is always grounded in the Bible as God's primary revelation and our ultimate truth-source.

**POWER OF GOD:** Processes and strategies will be ineffective unless we invite and embrace the presence and power of God. In order to experience community and growth, Jesus needs to be the centerpiece of our group experiences, and the Holy Spirit must be at work.

**REDEMPTIVE COMMUNITY:** Healing best occurs within the context of community and relationships. It's vital to see ourselves through the eyes of others, share our stories, and ultimately find freedom from the secrets and lies that enslave our souls.

**MISSION:** God has invited us into a larger story with a great mission of setting captives free and healing the broken-hearted (see Isa. 61:1-2). However, we can only join in this mission to the degree that we've let Jesus bind up our wounds and set us free. Others will be attracted to an authentic, redemptive community.

## HOW TO GET THE MOST FROM THIS STUDY

**1. Attend each Small-Group Experience.**
- Watch the DVD segment.
- Participate in the group discussion.

**2. Complete the material in this workbook.**
- Read the session and complete the activities before arriving to your next Small-Group Experience.
- Be honest with yourself and others about your thoughts, questions, and experiences as you study and apply the material.
- Ask God to show you His truth about each topic so that you can be confident you're following Jesus as the Lord of your life.

# ABOUT THE AUTHOR
## MIKE GLENN

Mike Glenn is the senior pastor of Brentwood Baptist Church in Brentwood, Tennessee. He is a gifted communicator with a passion to reach young adults and a unique ability to speak to any generation.

"When I was in seminary, I was told by a friend of mine that I could 'make change.' He told me, 'You can take these million dollar ideas we talk about in theology and break them down into 20s and 10s for everyone else to use.' And I guess that pretty much sums up my ministry as pastor. I can understand the big ideas of theology, but I have to be able to break them down so my people can use them in the places where they live. The local church has to make the great truths of our faith work in real life. Most of my ministry has been about 'making change.' I think any writing I do would do the same thing—help brothers and sisters understand the good news of the gospel in their current life setting."

Since Mike came to Brentwood Baptist in 1991, membership has skyrocketed from 900 to more than 8,500. Mike is also the teaching pastor of Kairos, a Tuesday-night worship service at Brentwood Baptist geared toward energetic young adults with a passion for growing in the Word of God. Attendance has grown to more than 1,000 in just a few short years. More can be learned about this ministry at *KairosNashville.com*.

Mike is a published author. His first book, *In Real Time: Authentic Young Adult Ministry as It Happens,* tells the story of Kairos. Mike's second book, *The Gospel of Yes,* was inspired by conversations he had with young adults at Kairos. You can read more from Mike on his blog, *mikeglennonline.com*. Follow him at *twitter.com/mikeglenn* and on *facebook.com/mikeglennonline*.

Originally from Huntsville, Alabama, Mike is a graduate of Samford University in Birmingham, and Southern Baptist Theological Seminary in Louisville, Kentucky.

Mike and his wife, Jeannie, live in Franklin, Tennessee. They have two married sons.

# INTRODUCTION

During the Italian Renaissance, artists discovered the illusion of perspective. By drawing lines that seemed to converge on the distant horizon, artists could add depth to paintings, theatrical staging, and even structures they designed and built. This discovery allowed them to portray the world much more realistically. By paying attention to scale, light and shadows in the coloring, and lines—either subtlety suggested or obviously shown—the artist could direct the viewers' eyes to the point of interest. How the artist used the illusion of perspective drew their attention to the point of significance.

Christ followers live in a complex, confusing, and ambiguous world. Technology has given us capabilities science fiction writers used to dream about. We communicate around the world at the speed of light. Social media brings us to events as they are happening. Our world is so fast that the morning paper is late. By the time the paper is printed, we've moved on to something else. If it's not now, it's late.

While our technology has opened up all kinds of possibilities in our world, it has also brought us to places we, literally, aren't wise enough to handle. Scientist are close to being able to clone human beings. The practice remains against international law, but some scientists are certain that this modern Frankenstein experiment is being attempted around the world today. Medical science has added years to our life span. Science has been so successful in keeping us alive that we have to ponder laws to help us decide when to end life. People are encouraged to have living wills with explicit instructions of what they want done in case circumstances no longer allow them to live certain ways. We can keep a body alive, but is  that the same as keeping a person alive? Most of us would agree that we're more than our physical bodies, but we would struggle to explain how.

What's the difference between our minds and our brains—our bodies and souls? What are those essential characteristics that make us human?

These questions and a thousand more like them are the realities confronting us in our everyday lives. Even mundane chores like emptying the trash become a tangle of ethical demands. Do we throw everything in the garbage or do we recycle? And if we recycle, how seriously should we recycle? If we're recycling, then should we compost?

See what I mean? Taking out the garbage shouldn't be this complicated.

Add to this the growing diversity of national culture and the problem becomes even more complex. Worldviews and individual assumptions have challenged the Christian consensus that existed from the end of World War II until the late 1960s. With the hyper individualism that began in the 1990s, pressing well into the 21st century, we have so many authorities, opinions, and experts, it's difficult to find a social consensus on questions of importance. Whatever view we might have on a particular issue, there will be those who take an opposing view. If it's not a clearly opposing view, it's likely one several shades different than our own.

Abortion is an obvious example. There are the expected opposing views of pro-life and pro-choice. Yet, within each position are several other positions of various interpretations. It's not unusual to find people who would agree on the big concept, but disagree about anything and everything else related to the question.

We live in a world of infinite possibilities, even when we're addressing important moral and ethical issues. For some questions, there just don't seem to be right or wrong answers. Worse, in other situations, there seem to be several right answers. Not only do good people disagree, *really* good people *really* disagree.

The thoughtful Christian who desires to follow Christ in every arena of life is then hit with a double whammy. A lot of the issues we face don't have a direct scriptural response. For some questions, indeed for a lot of questions, there's no "thou shalt not" text giving us unambiguous and direct guidance. For instance, we know murder is wrong. A commandment forbids it. But is that commandment binding in every circumstance?

What if someone breaks into your home intending to hurt you and your family?

"Well," you say, "that's different."

I know, but that's the point. It's a gray area.

So how do we deal with those gray areas? What about questions of ethics, morality, identity, or behavior that Scripture doesn't directly address? What about questions leading us to certain passages in the Bible that can be interpreted in more than one way?

For instance, does Jesus really expect us to turn the other cheek when we're struck by an enemy? Or is Jesus using hyperbole to make His point of expecting His followers to react non-violently?

What about when the Greek or Hebrew wording can lead us to interpretive shades of meaning within the same text? A lot of us would rather just avoid these difficult decisions, smiling as we say that questions like these are better off left to those people who are much smarter than we are.

One problem is even these smart people disagree. Another problem is that as much as we would like to avoid these issues, sooner or later we'll have to face them.

That's why we began our conversation with the idea of perspective. This vantage point from which we engage these questions before us will have a great deal of impact in determining how we address these questions. Perspective will determine what questions we answer, how we answer these questions, and how our answers will be woven into our lives. Join me as we explore some of these questions.

GRAY AREAS

# SESSION 1

*Is There Truth I Can Trust?*

# SMALL-GROUP EXPERIENCE

*Watch the corresponding video from the Teaching DVD,*
*then launch into the discussion guide below.*

### OPEN

Have each person come up with three statements about themselves, two being true and one being false. Take turns going around the room, sharing your statements. Make guesses as to which are true/false.

- *Who told the best lie?*
- *How easy was it to tell the difference between the truth and a lie?*

Truth vs. lie. Right vs. wrong. Good vs. evil. We can all agree that certain things are clearly good—like feeding the hungry or recycling. We can even agree that some things are inherently bad—like genocide, child trafficking, or racism. Yet many issues become less clear when we drill down below the surface. *Should I obey my parents if they're not Christians? How far is too far sexually with my boyfriend or girlfriend? Is it sinful to use bad language?* The Bible gives us guidance on each of these questions. And that leads us to the topic at hand—Is the Bible trustworthy? Pontius Pilate himself, the person responsible for ordering Jesus' crucifixion, mocked Jesus by asking Him, "What is truth?" (John 18:38).

### DISCUSS

- *How do you define truth?*
- *Is there a difference between facts and truth? Explain.*
- *Do you believe absolute truth exists or that truth is relative to each person's belief? How would you defend your answer?*
- *What difference would absolute truth make in your life?*

The Bible uses the word *truth* a minimum of 168 times. Here are the basic claims Scripture makes: God is real. He created the world and each of us. God chose to communicate with us through His divinely-inspired Word, the Bible. And God sent His only Son, Jesus, to die for our sins. So how can we know that Scripture is right? Countless arguments have been developed to support the validity of the Bible, but let's focus on just one: John Wesley, an 18th century theologian, said,

> "The Bible must be the invention either of good men or angels, bad men or devils, or of God. 1. It could not be the invention of good men or angels, for they neither would nor could make a book and tell lies all the time they were writing it, saying 'Thus saith the Lord,' when it was their own invention. 2. It could not be the invention of bad men or devils, for they would not make a book which commands all duty, forbids all sin, and condemns their souls to hell to all eternity. 3. Therefore, I draw this conclusion, that the Bible must be given by divine inspiration." —John Wesley and James Henry Potts[1]

Read 2 Timothy 3:16. If the Bible is God's Word—and we believe it is—then it is truth. We can count on it. It is trustworthy, valid, and timeless. Once we know the Truth, we can begin to apply it to our lives.

## APPLY
Read Psalm 16:11; Romans 8:28; and 1 Peter 3:18.

- *How do you respond to the fact that God seeks the best for you? How does that change your perspective on obeying and glorifying Him?*
- *What is God teaching you through this session?*
- *How will what you've learned affect your decisions throughout the next week?*

## PRAY
Transition to a time of prayer. Thank God for the provision of His Word, the salvation of His Son, and that we can know He is working for our good and His glory.

1. John Wesley and James Henry Potts, *Living thoughts of John Wesley* (Eaton & Mains, 1891), 413.

THE PARABLES OF JESUS AREN'T DESIGNED TO GIVE US NEW INFORMATION BUT RATHER TO GIVE US NEW STAINED-GLASS WINDOWS THROUGH WHICH WE VIEW GOD, OUR NEIGHBORS, AND THE WORLD AROUND US. THE PARABLES OF JESUS GIVE US NEW WINDOWS TO PLACE IN OUR MINDS AND SOULS SO WE CAN LITERALLY SEE IN A DIFFERENT WAY.

Perspective is important. As Christians we know this to be true because of the times we see Jesus developing the perspective of His followers. When you think about it, a lot of Jesus' teachings weren't so much direct commands as they were stories, insights, and questions designed to influence and shape our perspective.

Look at the types of questions we see Jesus asking:

> Why do you look at the speck in your brother's eye
> but don't notice the log in your own eye?
> *Matthew 7:3*

> What will it benefit a man if he gains the whole world
> yet loses his life? Or what will a man give in exchange
> for his life?
> *Matthew 16:26*

**Why do you call Me "Lord, Lord," and don't do the things I say?**
*Luke 6:46*

**If then you're not able to do even a little thing, why worry about the rest?**
*Luke 12:26*

**If I have told you about things that happen on earth and you don't believe, how will you believe if I tell you about things of heaven?**
*John 3:12*

As you've probably noticed, these were all rhetorical questions. Questions like these were intended to bring you to a fork in the road. You would either confront your faulty belief system or ignore the question altogether. These questions were designed to shape a certain perspective—leading to a deeper understanding of Christ's mission and our role in it.

**Why do you think the concept of perspective is important?**

**How can a proper perspective lead us toward a deeper understanding of our role in Christ's mission?**

**How is God currently trying to shape your perspective?**

## STAINED-GLASS WINDOWS

We used to think the mind worked like a filing cabinet. We were given information and we would assign it to a particular file in our mental cabinet. When we needed to retrieve the information, we would reach into the appropriate file and pull it out.

Now we understand the mind works much more like a picture gallery. We hold onto our memories not in lines of data but in images. If I ask you to think of an important day, say the day you got your driver's license, you don't think back on it as, *Roman numeral 1: I woke up. Roman numeral 2: I got dressed to get my license.*

No, you think back to the moment when you first saw your face laminated on the new card.

Most of our important memories in life are recorded as images. What makes these images both unique and important is they don't just hang on the walls of our minds for us to see and recall from time to time. Instead, these images work more like stained-glass windows we look through to view the world around us. The windows not only determine *how* we see the world, they filter *what* we see as well.

All of us have a mind full of these stained-glass windows we've constructed over our lives. We have pictures of all kinds of things: ourselves, Christ, the universe, our families, truth, and goodness—really everything we encounter in our world and in ourselves.

The reason these windows are so important is we literally view the world outside of us and everything within us through these stained-glass windows. These windows will both distort and enhance how we see the world around us. As a result, they will determine how we live in the world. In other words, if you want to change, you have to change the windows in your mind.

**Name three things a believer might view differently than a nonbeliever because they are seeing them through different stained-glass windows? (Ex. relationships, serving the poor, etc.) Explain the possible differences.**

1.

2.

3.

Knowing the *why* is often more important than knowing the *what.* This is why Jesus told so many stories. The parables of Jesus aren't designed to give us new information but rather to give us new stained-glass windows through which we view God, our neighbors, and the world around us. The parables of Jesus give us new windows to place in our minds and souls so we can literally see in a different way.

Take, for instance, the story of the Good Samaritan in Luke 10. According to Luke, an expert in the law asks Jesus how he can be sure he will find eternal life. Jesus asks the lawyer to quote and interpret the law. The lawyer replies by quoting the two great commands found in Matthew's Gospel:

> **Love the Lord your God with all your heart, with all your soul, and with all your mind. This is the greatest and most important command. The second is like it: Love your neighbor as yourself.**
> *Matthew 22:37-39*

Jesus agrees with the man and commends his interpretation. "Do this," Jesus says, "and you will live" (Luke 10:28).

The lawyer, being a good lawyer, wanted to clarify the terms of the commandments. How does Jesus define "neighbor"? In reading the conversation, you get the impression the lawyer was looking for an exact definition. For instance, our neighbors live on either side of our house and across the street, but if they live two streets over, they aren't our neighbors.

But Jesus does something interesting. He changes the question. The question for Jesus isn't, "Who *exactly* is my neighbor" but rather, "*Am I* a neighbor to those around me?" Jesus gave the lawyer a new window to look through. Jesus answered the question not by giving the lawyer new information, but by giving him a new perspective—a new way to see himself and the world around him.

**What are other examples in Scripture of Jesus giving new stained-glass windows to look through instead of more information and laws to live by?**

One example in Scripture was Jesus' continual dealings with blindness. Several of the miracle stories involve Jesus healing the blind. But as powerful as these stories are, the issue of blindness runs throughout the ministry of Jesus. There were those around Him who, for various reasons, either couldn't see or wouldn't see. They remained blind to the truth of who Jesus is. Healing blind eyes is more than recovering the ability to physically see; it's the ability to perceive and to understand how God is working in the moment. It's the ability to understand how God is thinking in a particular situation and then to align our choices and actions with His desires.

## GOD IS LOVE

One of the most important of those stained-glass windows in our minds is the image we have of God. I've always found it interesting that John, in his first letter to the local church, described God as love. First John 4:16 he writes, "God is love, and the one who remains in love remains in God, and God remains in him."

Here's what I find interesting about that passage. John could have chosen a lot of words to complete his thought. He could have said "God is holy." He could have written "God is righteous." Any of these words would have been right. Any of them would have given us a different insight into the character and person of God. But John chose *love*. Not only that, he chose a particular word for love that describes the essence of God—*agape*. There are three words used in the Greek language of the New Testament for love: *Eros* describes romantic love. *Phileo* is the word used for the love between friends. And *agape* is the word that's used to describe the love of God.

Here's the main difference. Agape seeks the best of the beloved—God's people—without looking for anything in return. Every action of God, every desire of God is summed up in this one word, *agape*. God has no other motivation. Creation, salvation, and even judgment is driven by a love determined to rescue the beloved.

**What's your reaction to the previous statement?**

**How is *agape* love different from the kinds of love we typically think of?**

This love in action surprised and impressed both the followers and enemies of Jesus. While trying to arrest Jesus, a soldier's ear was cut off by Peter. Jesus not only healed his ear, He also reprimanded Peter. To Peter's amazement—and everyone else's amazement—Jesus embraced the very soldier sent to arrest Him.

Jesus defended the woman caught in adultery and the woman who anointed His feet with nard in Simon's house. After the resurrection, Jesus told the women to tell Peter He was looking for His disgraced disciple. The apostle Paul was found on the road to Damascus on his way to persecute followers of Jesus.

Jesus was true to His own stories. He was the shepherd willing to leave the 99 sheep in the fold to go and look for the one lost sheep. The love of God compels Him to reach out to us who are lost. He doesn't wait on us to come to Him. God comes to us in Jesus Christ.

Most of us see a disconnection between love and truth. Truth is hard, unchanging, made of steel and concrete. On the other hand, love is seen as soft and unstable—an emotion that can't be trusted as a reliable guide for our lives. But with God, there is no such conflict. God is love. God is truth. They are both descriptions of His character and His essence.

In 1 Corinthians 13, Paul describes "love," but most of us would agree the "love" described by Paul in this familiar chapter is unlike any kind of love that we have known about. Paul introduces this chapter on love by telling the Corinthian church he will show them a "more excellent way."

The love Paul describes is:
- strong enough to bear all things.
- strong enough to overcome death itself.
- strong enough to give a second life to dying humanity.

This is a much different kind of love than the weak and sensitive love depicted by most cultural poets.

This is the love that defines the essence of God. This is the love that we'll see when we know God. This is the love that defines and motivates everything God desires and does.

God is love. Everything He does is done in this same love—creation, redemption, and the establishment of an eternal kingdom of our Lord Christ. This is the love shown to us in Christ Jesus.

**Are the ways Paul describes *love* difficult for you to believe? Which of the ways is most difficult for you to believe? Why?**

**How is this love Paul speaks of different—or a more excellent way than the love you have experienced from life's relationships?**

"In the beginning," John writes, "was the Word" (John 1:1). The Greek word *logos* can be interpreted as "meaning" also. "In the beginning was the *meaning*." And what was this meaning? This meaning was the essence of God—agape—Christ is the agape of God in human form.

The agape message Jesus taught to His disciples is what He knew from the Father. God-love, agape, is a love that always seeks the best for the beloved. God-love doesn't seek its own pleasure, but sacrifices itself for whatever the beloved needs. This is how Jesus teaches us to love our world.

## LOVING OTHERS

Jesus said there are two great commandments: "Love the Lord your God with all your heart, mind and soul" (Matt. 22:37). And the second is like the first: "Love your neighbor as yourself" (v. 39). According to Jesus, all of the teachings of the Law and the Prophets were contained in these two commandments.

Most of us can see how He established a triangle of relationships. The way Jesus laid out this teaching, a disciple can't keep one without keeping all three, and the three can't be kept without keeping each one. To love God requires us to love our neighbors, and we can't love our neighbors without authentically loving ourselves. In order to love ourselves, we have to know God's love in our own lives. Like the Trinity itself, these three commandments can't be separated if they are to be obeyed.

Look at how John puts it in his first letter:

> Dear friends, let us love one another, because love is from God, and everyone who loves has been born of God and knows God. The one who does not love does not know God, because God is love. God's love was revealed among us in this way: God sent His One and Only Son into the world so that we might live through Him. Love consists in this: not that we loved God, but that He loved us and sent His Son to be the propitiation for our sins. Dear friends, if God loved us in this way, we also must love one another. No one has ever seen God. If we love one another, God remains in us and His love is perfected in us.
>
> *1 John 4:7-12*

The story of the Good Samaritan tells followers of Christ to be aware of those who are wounded around us. When we see them, Christ wants us to take the initiative to bind up their wounds and care for them. We're to treat others in the same way Jesus, seeing us in our distress, healed our wounds and provided us a safe place to recover. In loving others, we return our love to Jesus. By taking care of the "least of these," Jesus says we are, in fact, offering a ministry to Him.

**Have you ever thought of loving others as synonymous with loving God? How should this impact our relationships?**

**How should this impact our interaction with the "least of these"?**

Being transformed into the likeness of Christ means we're transformed by and into the God-love agape. Our character is being conformed to the character of Christ. As He is filled with God-love, we also become filled with God-love. As a result, whatever circumstance confronts us, we respond with God-love.

Whenever we're squeezed by life, anytime we have to deal with a tough issue, we respond to that moment with the God-love of Christ.

Why? We do because it's what's in us.

If you squeeze a tube of toothpaste, toothpaste comes out. Why? Because that's what's inside. In the same way, whenever life knocks us around, it only knocks the love of Jesus out of us because that's all that's inside.

One reason Christianity is so difficult sometimes is because Christ never gives His followers permission to react. We're never allowed to act one way because somebody else acted another way first. We can't say to Jesus, "I'm sorry I lost my temper, but You should have seen what the other guy did."

Jesus *did* see what the other guy did, and as Christ followers, we only act out of obedience to Jesus, not in reaction to the actions of another. Jesus never gives us permission to disobey. We're always called to live out of the God-love Christ has put into our lives. The love of God, the essence of God, is to be our essence as well.

**Do you find this concept intimidating or difficult—to live out a God-love when life knocks us around? Why or why not?**

**Where, specifically, are you failing to live out this God-love in your relationships?**

**What does it mean that the essence of God should be our essence as well?**

What do you think when you hear, "What Would Jesus Do?" Many of us have worn these WWJD bracelets. The reason for this bracelet is for the wearers to see the initials and be reminded to think about how Jesus would respond to a particular situation before simply acting out our feelings.

More than thinking "What Would Jesus Do?" the believer needs to think through "Who Would Jesus Be?" That is, Christ followers should seek to become like Jesus to the point that we live out of His essence in us the way He lived out the essence of the Father before us. Like Christ, everything about us—our thoughts, our actions, our dreams and desires—must flow from our essence, which is agape, the God-love of Christ.

WOJD?
What Did Jesus Do?

## LOVING SCRIPTURE

The best way to know Jesus is through the study of His Word. Most of us assume this goes without saying, but if I've learned anything as a pastor it's that there isn't anything that goes without saying. Let me be plain. If you want to know Jesus, you have to love and study His Word. Notice I said "study," not "read." Christ's followers should cultivate a deep hunger and love to know the Scriptures. For in knowing the Scriptures, we know Christ Himself.

Reading the Bible for rules to live by is fine, but it's the shallowest way to read the Bible. We read the Bible, not so much to know the rules, but to know Christ. Think about it. When we open the Scriptures, we open this divine book in the presence of the Author and Subject of the book.

**Read Hebrews 4:12. How does the author of Hebrews describe the Word of God? How is this different than viewing the Bible as a set of rules to live by?**

Christ has given us His Spirit to walk beside us and guide us into all truth. As we encounter His Word, it shapes us more and more into His likeness—the same way His word formed the universe in creation. His heart becomes our heart. His thoughts become our thoughts. His desires are ours. We have been crucified with Christ and are now dead to our sins. It's not we who live, Paul reminds us, but Christ.

This is the divine perspective that allows us to find the wisdom of Christ in how we face the world. Following Christ, we engage the world in those places where brokenness and confusion rob lives of meaning and hope. We stand in the places where relativism and individualism muddle morality to a place where no one can understand it. This is the place we dig in. This is where we identify the gray areas and begin to speak truth into them. But as we speak this truth, we do it with a God-love in mind.

As Paul comments on this in Ephesians when he says,

> **Speaking the truth in love, let us grow in every way**
> **into Him who is the head—Christ.**
> *Ephesians 4:15*

See, it's not enough to be right; we have to be truthful and loving at the same time—and this is not easy.

 Agape is the perspective from which we view the world. God's love determines what we value, how we respond, and what actions we'll take and not take. Agape not only determines what questions we hear, but how we address them. Our answers, to be faithful to Christ, must come from the essence of God Himself—agape. The mystery of the faith, according to Paul, is the reality of Christ in us. Christ in us means agape in us. When the hard questions are asked, agape will be our answer. This is the good news of Jesus. Love is the essence of God—the essence of all that matters and lasts.

**When confronted with gray areas in the past, what has typically been your starting point or motivation in addressing these issues?**

**If we understand that agape is to be our perspective, our essence, and our answer, how should this reshape the way we approach gray areas?**

**How is studying Scripture with the love of Christ in mind different from studying with a motivation to find a specific answer? Give an example.**

In the end, there is no shortcut. In order to deal with these complicated issues of our post-modern culture, a disciple of Jesus must study Scriptures in the presence of the Divine Author so that the disciple understands not only the literal meaning of the text, but the heart of the One who gave us the text. For instance, what if we were able to understand the First Commandment as a command of mercy and grace?

Let me explain. When we first read the commandment, "Do not have other gods besides Me" (Ex. 20:3), the commandment sounds demanding and judgmental. But what if we were to understand this command is given to us because of God's love for us?

Another word for *glory* is *weight*. Scientists describe objects in terms of "atomic weight." An object has to have a certain weight to have the gravitational pull to hold everything else in orbit. What if God is saying to us He is the only One who has the "atomic weight" to hold our lives in their proper orbit? What if God is telling us that if we put anything or anyone else in the place where only He can be, our lives will spin out of control?

See the difference? Yes, there is a literal interpretation, but there is a deeper truth in the text as well. It's a truth based on the love God has for His children that, in turn, informs us how we're to react—not only to Him, but to the world around us.

Why does it matter that we work this hard in dealing with the complicated issues of our time? Because the salvation experience involves the total person: heart, mind, and body. Every aspect of our lives—the way we think, the things we desire, how and what we love—has been scarred and disconnected from God's intentions, and needs to be redeemed.

As Paul reminds us:

> **Do not be conformed to this age, but be transformed**
> **by the renewing of your mind, so that you may**
> **discern what is the good, pleasing, and perfect will**
> **of God.**
> *Romans 12:2*

One place the salvation process begins is with a renewal of our minds. A mind filled with Christ-formed stained-glass windows will see His kingdom purposes in our decisions and bring kingdom wisdom to these issues and others like them.

GRAY AREAS

# SESSION 2
## *Honor Code*

# SMALL-GROUP EXPERIENCE

*Watch the corresponding video from the Teaching DVD,
then launch into the discussion guide below.*

**OPEN**

Have everyone face each other in a circle. Take turns saying his or her name and something they've done that they think no one else in the group has done. If someone else has also done it, the person must state something else until he/she finds something no one else has done.

> • *How hard was it to find something that made you unique?*
> • *How are uniqueness and self-worth connected?*

**DISCUSS**

Read John 8:32 and Ephesians 3:17-19.

> • *What idols do we create that distract us from our God-given honor?*
> • *How does the world determine someone's value? How does that differ from God's definition of worth?*
> • *What attributes should a person of honor display?*
> • *Why do we often feel compelled to find our own worth from the approval of others? How can this be a positive thing? A negative thing?*

Ultimately, our value comes from God and no one else. We can forever seek the approval and acceptance of others, but it will be in vain. People are flawed and imperfect. We make mistakes. Yet God is perfect and created us to love Him and love others. Once we understand our own worth in Christ, we can show value and honor to others in a godly way.

**APPLY**

Read Matthew 22:36-40 and 1 John 4:9-11.

- *What implications do these passages have on our relationships with others?*
- *What does honor look like in your current relationships?*
- *With someone you're dating?*
- *With coworkers?*
- *With family?*
- *With strangers?*
- *How can you show honor to God?*
- *What steps will you begin this week? Read Isaiah 61:1-3 for inspiration.*

**PRAY**

Close with a prayer of thanksgiving that we don't need to find our worth in beauty, ability, intellect, or approval. Thank God that we find our value in Him alone. Pray for the ability to internalize what we've learned through this session and for the willingness to show honor to God and to all of His creation.

**WITH CHRIST, HONOR IS NOT EARNED. IT'S GIVEN. THE GOSPEL RESTORES DIGNITY LOST THROUGH SIN AND FAILURES. CHRIST GIVES BACK TO HIS FOLLOWERS WHAT THE FALL HAS TAKEN AWAY.**

Before we begin talking about some of the questions that prompted the discussion of gray areas—these things that challenge our living as Christ followers in our postmodern culture—we need to reclaim an often overlooked but integral aspect of the perspective Christ brings to us and from which calls us to live. This neglected teaching is the concept of honor.

**In your own words, briefly define the word *honor*.**

**Is there someone in your life who embodies the concept of honor? Name that person and explain why you feel that way.**

## HONOR EARNED VS. HONOR GIVEN

Honor means to "hold in high esteem." In our culture, honor is reserved for those persons who've achieved a remarkable feat or attained a certain status. An athlete is honored for winning championships. Michael Jordan is considered the greatest basketball player in NBA history because he won six championships. Business leaders are honored for having reached certain levels of success. Warren Buffet is held in high esteem because he's a billionaire. He's invited to talk to world leaders. He's given the best seat at the restaurant. And why not? He's earned it.

We also see a modern phenomenon of men and women being regarded as famous simply for being famous. However, most people would make a definite distinction between those who have earned the recognition of honor and those who simply have recognition—and did nothing to earn it. In street slang, we recognize the difference between "players" and "pretenders."

And that's the point of honor in our culture. Honor must be earned. You have to be willing to pay the price required to achieve the goal, and this price can be enormously high. Families are neglected, marriages are lost, and sometimes, personal injuries leave the champion with a lifetime of pain. I'm a big football fan, but honestly, when I see the price a number of childhood heroes paid to play the game, I'm not so sure it's worth it. Many of them limp with bad knees and hips, fingers are permanently dislocated, and studies are now revealing the permanent and debilitating damage concussions can cause. Whether an athlete, an artist, or anyone in the spotlight for that matter, the price of honor can be very high.

**Why do you think culture demands this kind of success to receive honor?**

**What's the difference between honor given to us by the world and honor given to us by God?**

**Mark on the following continuum the extent to which you typically are willing to receive honor from the world.**

**Only when it's convenient**                                          **At all costs**

|—————————————————————————————————|

Though it may seem obvious, we often forget that this honor given to our world's "heroes" is purely shallow at its core. If a team wins the Super Bowl they're the champions of the football world. But if a new team wins the following year another champion is named. The world just forgets about the previous champion. Entertainment is the same way. Release a great record and our world just wants another one. Star in a great movie and the world wants to know what's coming out next. Once honor has been given, the world demands an ever-rising level of success for one to keep the honor bestowed on them. Sometimes the person honored gets caught on this treadmill to the point when they regret ever having received the honor in the first place.

This is a fundamental difference between the teachings of Christ and the expectation of our world. With Christ, honor is not earned. It's given. The gospel restores dignity lost through sin and failures. Christ gives back to His followers what the fall has taken away. Honor is one of those things.

Look at Christ's words to His followers in the Gospel of Matthew:

**You are the salt of the earth. But if the salt should lose its taste, how can it be made salty? It's no longer good for anything but to be thrown out and trampled on by men. You are the light of the world. A city situated on a hill cannot be hidden. No one lights a lamp and puts it under a basket, but rather on a lampstand, and it gives light for all who are in the house. In the same way, let your light shine before men, so that they may see your good works and give glory to your Father in heaven.**
*Matthew 5:13-16*

Jesus doesn't tell His followers, "You can earn the right to be salt." Or, "I want you to earn enough points to become light." No, Jesus tells us we are light and salt—present tense. Our being salt and light is an honor given to us in our relationship with Christ. In the same way, Jesus called Simon Peter "the rock." Peter, however, was anything but stable in his commitment to Christ. Peter failed Jesus several times after this pronouncement, most infamously when he denied Jesus three times after Jesus was arrested.

Instead of waiting to reward our good behavior, Christ bestows the gift of honor on us at the beginning of our journey. We're called His children and given a vision of who we're created to be in His image. Our journey—our growth as disciples—is the process of aligning our lives with the revelation of who we are in Him. Since we've been honored by Christ, we're called to immediately begin to live in that honor.

See, no matter who you are or what you have done, you are someone of honor—not because of what you have done, but because you are a small picture of who God is.

**Reflect on the previous statement. Do you fully believe this? Is this how you perceive yourself? Why or why not?**

## THE GREAT ARTIST

Like great pieces of art, people are treasured not because of our inherit worth, but because we bear the imprint of the Artist. Martin Kemp is an art expert who lives just outside of Oxford, England. He is, however, not just any art expert. Kemp has become a leading scholar in the works of Leonardo da Vinci. With Kemp's approval, a piece of paper—a sketching or rough drawing—can suddenly be worth millions of dollars. Of course, without Professor Kemp's endorsement, a piece of art thought to be worth millions can suddenly become worthless. Kemp has spent more than four decades examining the details of da Vinci's work. When studying a painting, Professor Kemp is meticulous and detailed in his approach. He has become an expert in the pigments and glazes used by da Vinci. He knows the type of paper, the brushstrokes, and the subtle varnishes that mark the work of the Italian genius. He has seen so many authentic works by da Vinci that Kemp has learned to trust his initial reaction to a piece he's examining. Kemp says he can recognize an original da Vinci the way the face of an old friend is known.

What I find interesting about this story is the value of the art isn't determined by the value of the piece itself. On the contrary, the art is determined to be valuable because of the signature of the artist. The art piece in question can be a sketch, a painting, even a doodle in the margin of a notebook, but if da Vinci's hand touched it, the piece is worth millions.

In the same way, I've always found it interesting that God introduces Himself to us in the Scriptures as Artist. The opening chapters of the Bible are about all the things God creates. Genesis begins by celebrating the birth of our universe and everything in it. That means, like Professor Kemp, we study the habits and techniques of the Artist so we can recognize His work however it comes to us. We train our eyes to recognize the Master's work in creation. We can see His handiwork in the Scriptures. We see His fingerprints on the church. We experience Him ultimately and supremely in His Son, Jesus Christ.

And we recognize His work in each other—in humanity. The crowning moment in the creation story is the creation of humanity. The creation of Adam is described in great detail and is markedly different from the other moments of the Creation story.

> Then God said, "Let Us make man in Our image,
> according to Our likeness. They will rule the fish of the
> sea, the birds of the sky, the livestock, all the earth,
> and the creatures that crawl on the earth." So God
> created man in His own image; He created him in the
> image of God; He created them male and female.
> God blessed them, and God said to them, "Be fruitful,
> multiply, fill the earth, and subdue it. Rule the fish
> of the sea, the birds of the sky, and every creature
> that crawls on the earth." God also said, "Look, I have
> given you every seed-bearing plant on the surface of
> the entire earth and every tree whose fruit contains
> seed. This food will be for you, for all the wildlife of the
> earth, for every bird of the sky, and for every creature
> that crawls on the earth—everything having the
> breath of life in it. I have given every green plant for
> food." And it was so. God saw all that He had made,
> and it was very good.
> *Genesis 1:26-31*

In this passage, human beings are given authority over the rest of creation, permission to use creation for their own benefit and worth. We are given worth. We're not more valuable because we're beautiful or intelligent. We're valuable because we bear the image of God. In our being, we find the signs of the Great Artist's work. We're valuable because in some way, we reflect the glory of the Artist Himself.

This is why murder is wrong. Murder is not a crime simply because the life of another human being is taken. Murder is wrong because the Artist, in whose image human beings are made, is wounded by the attack on the life of another person. And the seriousness of this attack is made known in Genesis 9:6 when it states that "whoever sheds man's blood, his blood will be shed by man, for God made man in His image."

Bearing the image of God alone makes one a person of value—a person of worth. That, in and of itself, is enough. Yet we live in a culture obsessed with self-esteem. Parents will go to the most extreme measures to ensure their children feel good about themselves. The result has been the opposite of what was intended. People in our culture get the message they're only of worth when they meet certain expectations or check off certain accomplishments. In our culture, we're valued for what we do, not who we are. But the gospel message we preach—that Jesus Christ, God's only Son, gave His life for sinful humanity—paints a much different picture of our value.

> **For while we were still helpless, at the appointed**
> **moment, Christ died for the ungodly. For rarely will**
> **someone die for a just person—though for a good**
> **person perhaps someone might even dare to die. But**
> **God proves His own love for us in that while we were**
> **still sinners, Christ died for us!**
> *Romans 5:6-8*

We are valuable not because we have earned it. On the contrary, Paul said we were helpless and ungodly. We are valuable because of the price Christ paid for us through His substitutionary death on the cross. And we're now worth more than can be expressed. Therefore, the foundation of authentic human self-worth is wrapped up in these two biblical truths: humans were created in the image of God, and Christ died in our place.


## GIVING HONOR TO OTHERS

This fundamentally changes the way Christ-followers address their fellow human beings. Honor isn't simply reserved for those in positions of power or fame. Honor isn't given to a person because of some great achievement. Honor is given because as Christ-followers that's who we are and what we are commanded to do. For instance, a cup of water given to a thirsty person is seen as serving the

Lord Himself. Neighbors are to be loved. Why? Because our neighbors likewise bear the image of God and are people for whom Christ died.

**Where do you find yourself needing to be reminded of this truth the most?**

**Read Romans 12:9-21. Specifically, how are we to show love and honor to others?**

**Of all the commands in this passage, which do you find the most difficult to obey? Why?**

Christ commands His followers to be people who extend honor to all who may be around them. Wives are commanded to honor their husbands. In turn, husbands are to honor their wives. This honor is offered to the other whether or not the one extending the honor believes the person receiving it deserves to be honored. The fifth commandment tells children to honor their parents. Period. The parents don't have to be good parents or even good people, but they are still to be honored.

We honor our employers because Christ-followers are taught to do our work as if we're working for Jesus Himself. Because we know we are loved by Christ and because we've been bought by the high price of His life, we're free to focus our attention fully on Christ. We can offer our hospitality without needing anything in return.

The early church began to understand this concept more clearly after Peter told his story to the Jerusalem council in Acts 11. Peter described a dream and an encounter he had with a Gentile man named Cornelius. Peter was commanded in his dream, "What God has made clean, you must not call common" (Acts 10:15). Peter's view of Gentiles changed as he understood how God viewed Gentiles. As he told his story about how God was working throughout the Roman Empire in Gentile cities, the early church also understood that God is no respecter of persons. Indeed, salvation is a gift of grace, free to all. This fundamental understanding of the universality of the gospel message enabled the church to explode across the Roman Empire. Every human was the same in two fundamental ways: First, all were sinners in need of grace. Second, salvation is God's free gift in Jesus Christ to all who believe.

**Is this the gospel message you understand? If yes, how does your life give evidence of your understanding in regard to your relationships with other believers who are different than you?**

**What about in the relationships you have with unbelievers?**

As this message was proclaimed, people's lives were changed, and they received the promise of inheriting the kingdom of God as His children.

One of the first changes was the restoration of dignity to their lives. Symbolically, you see this in several stories of lame men being healed. The repeated command to "rise" or "stand up" is the call of Christ to all who follow Him to assume their full posture as heirs of the kingdom. In the same way, Paul encourages Timothy to be bold in his preaching because the young preacher was not given "a spirit of fearfulness, but one of power, love, and sound judgment" (2 Tim. 1:7). Living without shame or guilt, fully alive in Christ gives a person a new sense of authentic self-worth and inherent value. This divine dignity can't be earned or demanded. It can only be received in faith. We are people of value and dignity because Jesus says we are.

**If you are a Christian, have you always thought of yourself as having an authentic self-worth because of who you are in Christ?**

**When are you most likely tempted not to believe this? Why?**

## HONOR IN A POSTMODERN WORLD

Now, let's talk about why the concept of honor is so critical to us as we face the questions of faithful living in our postmodern world. Every person we meet is a person endowed with gracious honor. Regardless of who they are, where they've been, or even what mistakes they've made—they're still people created in the image of God and someone for whom Christ died. The radical teaching of the gospel is that because of God's great love for us, He made us alive in Christ even though we were considered dead in our own sin. God saw us valuable enough to send His Son to live a life we were incapable of living and die a death we should have died.

Look at how Paul describes it in Ephesians:

> **God, who is rich in mercy, because of His great love**
> **that He had for us, made us alive with the Messiah**
> **even though we were dead in trespasses. You are**
> **saved by grace! Together with Christ Jesus He also**
> **raised us up and seated us in the heavens, so that in**
> **the coming ages He might display the immeasurable**
> **riches of His grace through His kindness to us in**
> **Christ Jesus. For you are saved by grace through faith,**
> **and this is not from yourselves; it is God's gift—not**
> **from works, so that no one can boast. For we are His**
> **creation, created in Christ Jesus for good works, which**
> **God prepared ahead of time so that we should walk**
> **in them.**
> *Ephesians 2:4-10*

Can we imagine what would happen to our relationships in our world if we approached everyone we know with the basic understanding that each person is created in the image of God and worth the life of Christ on the cross? Do you know it was this understanding of the gospel message that was foundational to the Civil Rights Movement in the United States? In certain parts of the pre-Civil War South, preaching the gospel to slaves was against the law. The message that they were given freedom in Christ made slavery under Christian masters absurd.

So, what happens if we take the biblical teaching of honor and apply it to our daily lives? What if a young man understands that honor is to be part of his dating life? What if every young man understood the young woman he's dating bears the image of God (because she does) and is someone Christ died for (because she is)? What if a young man understood the young woman he is dating is loved by Christ and He has a plan for her life—a plan for her good and for the glory of His kingdom (because He does)?

Of course, what if every young woman thought the same way about the young man she was dating? I believe viewing our dating lives through the lens of biblical honor would have a significant impact in who we dated, what we did on our dates, and what we understood the purposes of those dates to be. The sad fact is this: the reality of Jesus rarely (possibly never) enters into our thinking about dating.

As Christians, this is just wrong. Jesus is Lord and He owns every aspect of our lives. Everything we do, including dating, should be done to honor Christ. With that understanding, we should at least understand we're not to do the person harm. We should leave them better. After being with a Christian young man or young woman, the person they have been dating should be closer to Christ and to His purposes for them.

But this doesn't happen. And the result? Reputations are ruined, hearts are broken, and future relationships are damaged. Once we have been treated with dishonor, how long does it take to trust again? And once we have started living with dishonor toward another, how do we flip the switch and start living with honor toward another?

Take a moment to consider these other important questions:

**How differently would we live if we understood we bear the image of God and are people deemed worthy of the suffering death of Christ on the cross?**

**What are the kinds of things we do over the course of our lives that dishonor us and the Lord we serve?**

**What would change in our own lives if we made the simple decision to treat ourselves with honor? What about treating others with honor?**

**How do we sometimes inflict pain on someone else because we mistakenly believe that we can move the pain from our lives to someone else?**

**If we make the other person hurt, will we relieve our own pain? What is often the result of this action?**

If we began by honoring ourselves, by keeping the Great Commandments to love our neighbors as we love ourselves, our world would be a markedly different place.

When you understand you have something in you that no one or nothing can take from you, then you can honor your boss, parents, friends, or enemies. Why? Because you've got too much Jesus in you to hold in one life. Some of it is going to spill out on that jerk of a boss you have. You can't hold the ocean in a thimble. It's going to spill out on your parents who disappointed you or who hurt you. It's going to spill out on friends who betrayed you.

Honor them. Why? Because you have been honored.

The Father knew my name before I was born. You can't take that away from me. That's how much I am worth. That's how much you're worth.

**Does the life you're living now reveal the honor that has been given to you? Why or why not?**

The choices you're making should be choices of a person of honor. You bear the image of the Artist who created you. You are paid for with an unspeakable price—so honor everybody. How in the world can you do that? Jesus has honored you and me first. Part of it is what you have been taught to think about yourself. And if you're not worthy of honor, if you don't feel honored, then it's hard to see that anybody else would be worthy of honor. You're always trying to tear somebody down rather than lift them up—because you're trying to make them feel the same pain that you feel. You think you will feel better, if you can just take your pain and do something with it to make somebody else hurt. But you can't move your pain to another person.

Now you can begin to see why this is so important.

There's a lot of talk these days of theology and science, about creation or evolution. What people don't understand about this is if you're a cosmic accident, if you're a bunch of proteins that happened to get together at the same place at the same time, if you don't bear the image of God—then where does honor come from?

Why do we relate any differently than the shrubs and trees in the yard, that happen to be another group of cells that got together at the same place? See how dangerous that becomes? There are some strong implications if we allow this worldview to go unchecked. Do we confront this worldview? If so, how can we do it with honor while confronting those we disagree with?

Perhaps some words from Peter will help us. He writes in 1 Peter:

> **Submit to every human authority because of the Lord,**
> **whether to the Emperor as the supreme authority**
> **or to governors as those sent out by him to punish**
> **those who do what is evil and to praise those who do**
> **what is good. For it is God's will that you silence the**
> **ignorance of foolish people by doing good. As God's**
> **slaves, live as free people, but don't use your freedom**
> **as a way to conceal evil. Honor everyone. Love the**
> **brotherhood. Fear God. Honor the Emperor.**
> *1 Peter 2:13-17*

**Is it difficult to live honorably in front of those who have opposing worldviews? Why or why not?**

**Are there teachers, employers, peers, neighbors, family members, or even friends who need to see Jesus spilling out of you? List three people who you will begin to honor because of the honor that's been given to you by God.**

**1.**

**2.**

A lot of times, we think the early Christians had it easier than we have it, that somehow being in the Middle East close to the time of Christ made it easier to be a believer. Not so.

The early church struggled for its survival in the most hostile of situations. How did they learn to thrive in such conditions? They lived honorably. They honored God. They honored each other. They honored their parents and their employers. Or, even more radical, if they were slaves, they honored their masters as if the masters were Christ Himself. Over time, this way of approaching life made an impression. People began to pay attention. They began to wonder themselves what it would be like to know how much they were worth in Christ Jesus and to live the life He gave them for all it was worth.

How we address the questions in the gray areas will directly be affected by what we think of God, ourselves, and each other. If we respond with honor toward all involved, we'll get closer to finding the kingdom answer in the question being asked.

GRAY AREAS

# SESSION 3

*Addiction*

# SMALL-GROUP EXPERIENCE

*Watch the corresponding video from the Teaching DVD, then launch into the discussion guide below.*

## OPEN

Have the group stand in a circle for a quick game of juggling. You'll need to provide several balls for this game. To begin, the person with a single ball tosses it to the person across the circle saying his/her name, and then puts his hands behind his back. This repeats until everyone has been tossed the ball and had his or her name said. Then repeat the pattern, with each group member throwing to the same person as before, but this time with a second ball. Continue the game, adding a new ball for each round. Continue the game until someone messes up.

- *What was most difficult about the game?*
- *In your opinion, what's the key to keeping the ball moving?*

Life can be similar to this game. Things move smoothly until there are too many things to juggle. School, work, friends, family, finances, to-do lists … we all get overwhelmed at times. However, when life gets complicated, we might turn to alternative sources of comfort—sources that can lead to addiction.

Take technology for example. Scan any coffee shop or mall and you'll find tons of people paying more attention to their phones than to those around them. It seems we've lost the ability to communicate face to face. As much as interpersonal communication is needed, more serious addictions have been plaguing us inside and outside the church for centuries.

## DISCUSS

- *How did the video give hope for overcoming weaknesses?*
- *If addiction is so destructive, why are so many people ensnared by it?*
- *What factors push people toward addiction?*
- *How can addiction, when left uncontrolled, destroy a person's life?*

Prescription drugs, marijuana, sex, shoplifting, and even online gaming or credit cards—our society is consumed by the need for entertainment, comfort, and pleasure.

GRAY AREAS

- *How can we tell when we've crossed the line between in control and out of control? Is personally discerning the difference possible? Explain your response.*
- *How are addictions a form of idolatry?*
- *Do you believe all addictions are sinful? Why or why not?*

Let's explore the connection between fear and addiction. Use a concordance to look up the word *fear*. If you don't have a concordance on hand, there are multiple online concordances you can use.

- *Why is fear so powerful?*
- *Read Joshua 1:9; Psalm 27:1 and 2 Timothy 1:7. What can we learn from these verses?*
- *Why is it hard to listen to God when He tells us not to fear?*

## APPLY

If we can overcome our fear and trust in the work of Christ in our life, then our past mistakes and concerns won't define our future. We can begin to heal. Read 1 Corinthians 10:13; Lamentations 3:22-23; Galatians 5:1 and Romans 6:6-7.

- *What do these verses teach about addiction, healing, and grace?*
- *Share a time when you've seen someone overcome his or her addiction.*
- *What potential pitfalls can you identify for the addictions you've discussed today? What safeguards can we put in place to avoid these dangers?*
- *Why do we still sin even after becoming Christians?*
- *Mike mentioned ways to overcome those setbacks. What other ways can you think of to keep moving forward?*

## PRAY

Break into groups of two. Take time to share with each other the good and bad addictions in your life. Discuss ways to avoid and/or overcome those addictions. Then pray for each other to close the session.

**IT'S NOT GOD'S WILL FOR YOU TO LIVE OR DIE BEHOLDEN TO ANYTHING BUT HIM. GOD DOESN'T WANT YOUR LOYALTY TO GO TO ANYONE ELSE BUT HIM.**

My favorite novel is *To Kill a Mockingbird* by Harper Lee. It's about a small town lawyer in Alabama who defends an African-American man who is wrongly accused of rape. Atticus Finch has kids, Jem and Scout. In the course of the book, Jem tears up Mrs. Dubose's camellia bushes. For his punishment, Jem has to read to her every afternoon. She is old, she is dying, she was the cranky, nosy neighbor, and Jem doesn't like being there at all. While he doesn't like it, he complies and reads the book every afternoon until a timer goes off. For the life of him, Jem can't understand why he has to do this.

A little later, Mrs. Dubose dies and Atticus explains to Jem why he was over there. Mrs. Dubose was fighting an addiction to morphine. And as long as Jem was reading, she could pay attention to what Jem was reading, fight the addiction, and not give in. So every time he read, they would stretch the time out—a little longer and a little longer—until she was able to withstand the craving for morphine and be free of her addiction to it. Atticus explained to his son Jem that she didn't want to die "beholden to anything."

That's an interesting phrase isn't it? She didn't want to die beholden to anything.

**In your own words, what do you think it means to be beholden to something?**

It's not God's will for you to live or die beholden to anything but Him. God doesn't want your loyalty to go to anyone else but Him. The Bible talks about God being very jealous over us the way a husband is jealous for his wife's attention. Many times people misread that and think behaviors like jealousy are beneath God. We know jealous people and they aren't attractive. So why would God act like that?

**Read the first two commandments from Exodus 20:3-6. What do these verses tell you about God's jealousy?**

The reason we often misunderstand this concept is we see it coming from an angry and judgmental God. We can't understand the command to have no other gods before Him is given out of God's mercy. God is the only One who can hold your life together. If you put anything or anyone else in the center of your life, your life will fall out of control. That's why He insists on being there. It's not out of jealousy or His ego. It's given to us in mercy.

This session is about addiction. Before we go on, I want you to hear me. You might be dealing with pretty tough stuff, and I'm not a doctor. We're going to be dealing with the spiritual aspects of addiction, which is important, but there are also physical realities when you are addicted to certain things. And you need to be treated physically.

If you're addicted to cocaine, you need to be under a doctor's care. If you're dealing with alcohol addiction, you need to be under medical care. Most addictions have a process to walk you through the physical aspects of the addiction before you can begin to deal with the spiritual and emotional aspects of the addiction. In fact, you likely know of people who have done pretty well dealing with the physical aspects of addiction, and then, when they have to deal with the spiritual and emotional pain that drove them to addiction in the first place, they'll relapse.

If you're an addict, you can choose anything (or sometimes something chooses you) to help you deal in an unhealthy way with your pain. It could be cocaine. It could be alcohol, sex, pornography, or work. People are even addicted to the Internet. It could be that you use food to self-medicate in order to ease the pain that you're feeling. It could be any number of things. Whatever your drug is— we're simply going to call it the "drug of choice."

**Is there anything you're aware of that you have become beholden to? If so, what is it?**

**Have you ever pondered whether of not this may be an addiction?**

I don't want you to read this and think I have it all together. I don't. Many of the things I'm writing about I've learned the hard way. And everyone deals with this temptation in one way or another. Our lives are filled with pain. We hurt. We're tired of hurting. We want to find something to make the pain go away.

## A CASE STUDY ON THE CHURCH IN GALATIA

The church in Galatia was Paul's problem child. He usually begins his letters with "I, Paul, apostle of Jesus Christ, saved by the mercy ... ." Next he gives a little bit of his testimony. Then he usually says, "To the saints," followed by describing the churches. Finally he gives some kind of blessing to whom he is writing.

However, he shortened his normal pleasantries with the church in Galatia. Listen to the language he uses at the beginning of his letter:

> I am amazed that you are so quickly turning away
> from Him who called you by the grace of Christ and
> are turning to a different gospel—not that there is
> another gospel, but there are some who are troubling
> you and want to change the good news about the
> Messiah. But even if we or an angel from heaven
> should preach to you a gospel other than what we
> have preached to you, a curse be on him! As we have
> said before, I now say again: If anyone preaches to
> you a gospel contrary to what you received, a curse
> be on him! For am I now trying to win the favor of
> people, or God? Or am I striving to please people? If
> I were still trying to please people, I would not be a
> slave of Christ. Now I want you to know, brothers, that
> the gospel preached by me is not based on human
> thought. For I did not receive it from a human source
> and I was not taught it, but it came by a revelation
> from Jesus Christ.
> *Galatians 1:6-12*

Paul asks them, "Who is messing with you?" That's where he starts. "Who has messed with you? They've gotten you off track. You started so well. Now I don't even know where you are."

He reminds them of the gospel that he preached about Jesus Christ being sent from God to die for sinners. It's the price that sin required, and that's the only price. It's the only price that can be paid for sin. You can't add anything to it, or you can't take anything away from it. That is the gospel.

**The word, *gospel*, is often tossed around in Christian settings and Christian conversations. How would you define *gospel*?**

**How has the truth of the gospel in Christian culture today been twisted or perverted?**

In Paul's time, there was a group of people in Galatia who came behind him and said, "If you really want to be a Christian, you have to do these other things too." And they brought in the Jewish Laws and said you have to keep the Laws of the Old Testament. You have to keep the dietary laws. You have to keep all the religious laws.

So all of a sudden, the church in Galatia that was free from the Law in Christ is now trying to behave and keep all the rules. They gave their power over to the keeper of the rules, because there was always somebody totaling up the points.

"Minus one, you didn't do that well. Plus one, you did that well."

It was always a matter of points.

"I've got to have enough points for today or I won't be a good-enough Christian."

It's like somebody was determining what "cool" was. But Paul didn't get that memo. He wasn't at that meeting. He didn't know who those people were or who determined the cool factor, but there was always somebody keeping points. Paul writes the defense, simply stating it's Jesus and Jesus alone.

Let me remind you of a fast way to find heresy—false teaching. Any time you hear the words, "Jesus and ..." or "Jesus or ...," you're into heresy. Anybody who says you have to believe "Jesus and ...," says that the suffering and death of Jesus wasn't enough. That's heresy. Anybody who says "Jesus or ...," says there's another way. Jesus told us there is only one way.

Now I know, in our day of political correctness I'm not supposed to say that. I'm supposed to claim there are lots of ways. There are many paths. But I didn't say Jesus is the way—Jesus did. And the reason we listen to Him is He is the One who came from God to us. Did you get that? If He came from God to us, He must be the One who knows the way back, from us to God. Make sense? He left His throne in heaven, came to earth, and says, "I can take you back." I am trusting Him to do that. Nobody else has done that.

In Galatians 5 Paul is beginning to wrap it up, to hammer home his argument. He says that "Christ has liberated us to be free. Stand firm then and don't submit again to a yoke of slavery" (v. 1).

Why were we liberated?

For freedom. To be able to live as a free man and a free woman in Christ—beholden to nothing. Paul explains that he has learned to be content in everything. Despite the situation, he remains a free man, not beholden to anything. Standing firm. Not submitting (see Phil. 4:11-13).

**What is it that motivates you to stand firm, not submitting to the thing that is trying to control you?**

**Is there truth you remind yourself of that helps you through these times? If so, what is it?**

You were released from bondage by the resurrection of Christ to live a free life in the resurrection that He brings to you. Don't give it away for the false security of slavery again. Yet this happened over and over again to God's people.

Look in the Old Testament. God brought Israel out of Egypt, into the promised land. Then right after Joshua died, they were slaves again. Read the stories in the Book of Judges. Joshua dies, the people forget who God is, and God allows them again to be carried away into slavery. One generation forgets all that God has done, and now they're slaves again.

But these stories didn't just happen in Old Testament times. It may take different forms, but it's still happening to God's people today.

## CONSEQUENCES

Responsibility leads to choices. Choices lead to consequences. Now let's not panic. There are good consequences, and there are bad consequences. And even some of the bad ones aren't really bad. Also, every bad choice isn't a sin. If you're learning to ride a bicycle and you fall over, that's not a sin. This happens in life. Sometimes it's not sin—you just make a bad choice. But sometimes it is sin.

There are consequences to choices, and with consequences comes pressure. What if I make the wrong choice? Or worse, what if I make the right one? How do I handle failure? What are my family and friends going to think? What about next time?

That pressure can lead to many different questions and concerns. And the anxiety from it all can create a huge hole in your heart. It's a hole that hurts a lot. It can cause you to act in all manner of ways.

- Failure can cause you to act out of anger.
- Failure can cause you to act out of resentment.
- Failure can cause you to be bitter.

And everyone has this. No one gets through life without it. All of us have been wounded. All of us have been rejected. All of us have been betrayed. All of us have been let down. We all carry these wounds, no exceptions.

**How do you handle pressure? What about failure?**

**On the continuum below, record where you typically find your acceptance.**

Needing continual
approval from others

Constant recognition
of acceptance in Christ.

**What wound is present in your life because of rejection or betrayal?**

So how do you deal with it? Here's where it gets dicey. If I'm going to deal with it in the freedom Christ has given to me, it may hurt worse before it gets better. When I ask Jesus to help me with a problem, I want Him to grab me and throw me on the other side of it. I want to look back and say, *Whew. That was a close call.* That's not what He does. He takes you right back to the problem, right back to the place it happened. And you begin to deal with it, little bit by little bit, but not by yourself—He's always there with you. The good thing about Jesus and the resurrection is that He's not bound by space or time, so He can go back to the past where you were hurt and take you with Him so you can understand it better. You'll be able to think through it, and hopefully get to the place where you say one of the following:

- This is my fault. I take responsibility and ask forgiveness for this.
- This was not my fault. I'm releasing it. I'm not going to carry it.
- This was true and I'm going to learn from it.
- This was not true and I'm rejecting it.

It's a slow, painful process, but it's the only redemptive way to deal with it. Why? So you're never afraid of it again. If Jesus grabs you and throws you on the other side of it, then you'll be afraid it will catch you later—that somehow you'll wake up and it's in your closet, ready to scare you once again. You'll always be afraid.

**Read through the following passages and record how each addresses your fears and anxieties.**

**Isaiah 41:10**

**Hebrews 4:14-16**

**1 Peter 5:6-7**

**1 John 4:18**

When Jesus walks you back through it in the power of the resurrection, you face it, deal with it, and He gives you victory over it. You won't be afraid of it anymore. When it rears its head or when someone brings it up, you can own it.

Someone may walk up to me and say, "Hey, I heard some things about you when you were in college, Mike."

"Yeah, you probably did."

"Were you the guy who ... ?"

"Yes I was. Not proud of it, but that was me."

So I deal with it. I'm not proud of it, but that was me. And I don't have to be afraid of it, because if Jesus isn't holding my sins against me, it doesn't matter who else is. You get that? Jesus looks at me and says, "We've talked about that. OK? It's over."

But for some reason we don't like that because we don't think it's enough—so we pick a drug. Now this drug can be porn, cocaine, alcohol, sex; you name it. There are all kinds of addictions, and you might be thinking, "Hey, that's mine." All of these are what we call the "drug of choice." It could be anything. And their control over us operates in similar ways.

We call pornography an addiction because your brain reacts the same way that it does when you ingest cocaine. The same kind of feel-good endorphins in your brain are released. This helps you feel better about yourself. That's why you get hooked on it, because you want to create that good feeling again and again and again and again, to the point that you will reject a real relationship for the illusion of pornography. All these drugs do the same thing. They are all diseases.

## A DISEASE

The reason we call addiction a disease is because it has a predictable course. We know what's going to happen. We know the drug will begin to pull you away from your relationships. You will walk away from people who don't help you use your drug. You'll sacrifice your education, your job, your friends, your marriage, and your children for your addiction. This is what addiction does.

But that's not the end of it. It takes more and more of the drug to keep you high and the pain off of your mind. It doesn't matter what drug it is—cocaine, alcohol, pornography—they all eventually stop working and it takes more and more "medication" to keep the pain away. The only thing that matters now is getting your next drug. And you know all of those lines you said you wouldn't cross? You will eventually.

**Have you ever crossed the line, doing something completely irrational, just to medicate your pain? If so, what led you to that point?**

**Did you feel in control of the situation or more like the situation was controlling you? Explain.**

You might say, "Oh. Hold on, Mike. I'm in control of this. I won't ever cross that line."

Yes you will.

The pain will drive you to more and more medication. And eventually you'll go to rehab. You'll go through detox and you'll start feeling better. Once the drug gets out of your system, guess what? All this pain you've been trying to avoid—it's waiting right there for you. Now, not only do you have to deal with the pain but also the damage caused by your addiction.

## PAUL'S PLEA

Paul wrote some pretty important stuff in Philippians. What about this passage?

> **Don't worry about anything, but in everything,**
> **through prayer and petition with thanksgiving, let**
> **your requests be made known to God. And the peace**
> **of God, which surpasses every thought, will guard**
> **your hearts and minds in Christ Jesus.**
> *Philippians 4:6-7*

You've heard this. It's one of those passages we hear but never really listen to. Read it again.

So how do you deal with worry? How do you deal with all the painful and unanswered questions? By understanding that Christ is your Savior, because He is your Lord. He is your friend, your High Priest, your big brother, the oldest member of your family. You belong to Him, and He belongs to you. You will be anxious about nothing. If you fill your life with Jesus, anxiety and pain is pushed out.

The thing I love about Paul is he always deals with real life. People talk about him being a theologian or a writer—he's a pastor. He's always dealing with real people in real life situations. So here's what he says for you to do. "Don't worry about anything." But what do I do with the anxiety?

Paul says, "Everything, through prayer and petition with thanksgiving, let your requests be made known to God."

Here's where most of us fail. We rank stuff in your lives by what we can handle and what we think Jesus should handle. There are things we pray about and there are things we just do. I know Paul said pray about everything, but that had to be an exaggeration. Right? We would never get anything done.

Sure, Paul is using hyperbole here, but not as much as you might think. Too many of us look at things in our lives and say we don't need to pray about this or that, and then we get into trouble. Remember, Paul also says to pray without ceasing (see 1 Thess. 5:17). Our prayer doesn't end with "amen" in the morning. We have the privilege of being in conversation with Jesus throughout the day. If He knows the number of hairs on our heads, then there's no detail that's too small to be part of our prayer lives. We are in constant conversation with Jesus, all day long, about every aspect of our lives. Everything is under His lordship and belongs to Him. That means we should be talking to Jesus about it.

**How much conversation with Christ do you have throughout the day?**

**What distractions draw your attention away from your Savior?**

Paul's plea also means we need to be studying Scripture. Paul tells us to dwell on those things that are true, honorable, just, pure, lovely, commendable (see Phil. 4:8). We need to know as much as we can about Jesus and fill our minds and hearts with a scriptural vision of Christ. From that vision, we need to add to our lives those things Jesus has in His life that we don't have in ours. On the other hand, we need to get rid of those things in our lives we have that aren't part of Jesus' life. In several places in his letters, Paul talks about putting off the old self of the flesh and putting on the new self in Christ (see Eph. 4:22-24). This is the process of daily dying to ourselves and coming alive in Christ. And this is exactly what Christ demands of us in order to be His followers.

Jesus described this very idea to His disciples in the Gospel of Matthew:

> If anyone wants to come with Me, he must deny
> himself, take up his cross, and follow Me. For whoever
> wants to save his life will lose it, but whoever loses
> his life because of Me will find it. What will it benefit a
> man if he gains the whole world yet loses his life? Or
> what will a man give in exchange for his life?
> *Matthew 16:24-26*

**What does it mean to take up your cross?**

To take up your cross means to put yourself in the place of a condemned criminal. But not just any condemned criminal—Jesus. He is saying "If I died, then you did too. To be My disciple, identify with My cross. And when you do this, you are identifying with Me and I with you."

You're a condemned criminal in the court of God. You are guilty of treason. You are guilty of abandoning the God who made you and loves you. You are guilty of infidelity. You cheated on the One who loves you more than you can understand. So graciously, Christ comes to you asking you to die to yourself and to the things that are preventing you from identifying with Him.

See the way we deal with our fears, pains, and anxieties is to first identify ourselves with Christ.

## HEALING PROCESS

We also deal with our fears, pains, and anxieties by allowing Jesus to heal them through prayer, Bible study, worship, and fellowship with other believers. Now, I know that sounds simplistic, but in reality it's not. Our time in prayer is a time of honest self-appraisal, going over the things in our lives that we're doing well, not doing well, things we're struggling with, and things we're afraid of. There's a strength that comes from our confession in the presence of the Savior who died for us. Words can't really explain the strength that comes from this kind of prayer.

Reading in Scripture the promises of Christ and seeing how He dealt with His disciples gives us confidence to live faithfully through the challenges of our lives.

Again in Philippians, Paul writes about the peace of God. We think of peace as the absence of war. In the Bible, peace means wholeness—completeness—finished. We're at peace. We're complete.

Paul writes that God will send His peace to surround and to equip our hearts. He will send the troops of peace to occupy our hearts, so that when anxiety attacks, it will be the peace of God that fights it back.

That's a different kind of peace, isn't it? This peace of God defends, attacks, and pushes back anxiety. It will guard our hearts, so that we're not anxious in our desires. And it will guard our minds, so we're not anxious in our thoughts. We won't have to hide the pain again in some addiction that could take over our lives.

**What kinds of protection can you set up now to prepare and guard your heart against Satan's attacks?**

**Does this sense of peace give you a feeling of freedom? Why or why not?**

Addiction is easy. You become a slave. You don't have to make any decisions if you're a slave. The decisions are made for you. Somebody else owns you. Somebody else tells you what to do. Somebody else tells you when to get up. Somebody else tells you when to go to bed. Somebody else tells you what to do all day.

But you weren't created to be that way or live that way. It's for freedom that you were set free. And right now, God is calling you to that free life. Now all of us are on this scale somewhere. You may think, *Well, thank God I'm not like that guy who's on Death Row or in rehab.* But all of us are dealing with anxiety in some kind of way, and a lot of us are dealing with it in unhealthy ways.

Perhaps this is the thing you've been afraid of most of all, that somehow you'd be caught, somehow you'd be ambushed, and you'd have to face it. Maybe for you, this is a bad place, because you're remembering the betrayal, the rejection, the failure, and how worthless you felt.

Maybe all that pain is very real to you today. In fact, you may be fighting the need to find your drug of choice. And you may already be thinking of getting a drink, shooting a line, or getting on the website *www.messmylifeupbeyondall-recognition.com.* Maybe you're thinking, *If I could just get out of here, I won't ever have to deal with it.*

But sooner or later you'll have to deal with it. Jesus died to give you your freedom. He doesn't want you to be a slave to anything. You're created and called to live in His freedom. Right now, Jesus wants you to be free from everything and to live "beholden" to nothing. He wants to bring healing to your heart, and peace to your anxieties. He is Lord. His is King, and He wants His people to live free.

GRAY AREAS

# SESSION 4

*Dating*

# SMALL-GROUP EXPERIENCE

*Watch the corresponding video from the Teaching DVD, then launch into the discussion guide below.*

## OPEN

Gather on a starting line next to the facilitator. Your goal is to cross the established finish line before anyone else by truthfully answering questions about yourself. The facilitator will make a statement (examples: I have blue eyes. I speak two languages.). If it applies to you, take one step forward. If it is false, remain on the starting line. The facilitator will ask another question, repeating the game until a winner is declared.

Games are fun to play, but in real life, discerning the truth about other people isn't always as easy—especially in relationships. Relationships take time to develop. We prove ourselves and our intentions to others over the course of many shared experiences.

- *When have you seen this to be true in relationships you have had?*

## DISCUSS

There's no more of an intimate experience with another person than sexual intercourse. It merges the souls of two people and can be a gratifying, wonderful gift within its God-given context.

- *What did you think of Mike's description of souls ripping apart when unmarried couples have sex?*
- *Did anything else stick out to you from Mike's discussion?*
- *Do you remember having "the talk" with a parent or other adult growing up? How did that go?*
- *What lessons have you learned from the church about dating and sex?*
- *How does our culture tell us to treat sex?*
- *How would you summarize God's plan for dating, marriage, and sex?*
- *What principles about dating, marriage, and sex can you infer from Scripture?*

## APPLY

- Read Proverbs 5:15-20. What does this passage tell you about God's plan? Does anything surprise you?
- What are the consequences of not following God's plan?
- How does this passage affect the way you view dating?
- If someone has made mistakes in the matters of dating and sex, how can he or she get back on track with God's plan?
- Mike spoke of having a mental picture of a future spouse. What might the benefits of having this image be? The drawbacks?
- What characteristics might you be looking for in another person? How can you develop those same characteristics within yourself?
- If you're already married, what advice can you give to dating couples?

## PRAY

Close in prayer. Thank God that He has a plan for sex and ask for His guidance for dating relationships. Ask for forgiveness for when we've failed Him, and for His help as we identify our future goals and dreams.

**EVERY RELATIONSHIP IS A GIFT. WE DON'T EARN THEM OR DESERVE THEM. CHRIST GIVES THEM TO US, LIKE EVERYTHING ELSE IN OUR LIVES, FOR OUR ENJOYMENT AND TO HELP US BECOME MORE LIKE HIM.**

I realize you might not be free to date. You might be married, or close to it. Or you might be in a position where dating isn't God's best for you right now. Whatever it may be, this lesson and the principles within it can still be applied to your life.

**On the following continuum, mark how you feel about the dating process, whether that was several years ago or right now.**

Easy breezy                                                    Like pulling teeth

├────────────────────────────────────────────────┤

**Why do you think dating is so difficult or easy for you?**

**From your perspective, what is or what was the most frustrating thing about dating?**

## TWO-SIDED COIN

Because of your stage in life you may not understand this, but nothing induces fear faster in any father's heart than the thought of his daughter dating. From the first moment he realizes he has a daughter to the moment the first boyfriend shows up at the front door, the father is worried about everything from who will ask her out to what kind of rules he'll have to enforce for her. Whatever else may happen, this dad is slowly beginning to realize he'll never get another good night's sleep in his life.

Of course, his daughter is worried for other reasons. Will the right young man ask her out? What will they do on their first date? Will he want to kiss her on the first date? Should she? And if she does kiss on the first date, what kind of girl does that make her?

But dating doesn't get any easier when you get to college and post-college, does it? Adding to the confusion is a culture that encourages young men and women to become sexually active as soon as they feel they're ready. The movies, songs, and television shows targeting these audiences assume young adults are sexually active. This only complicates the already complex and confused issue of dating.

**Where do you see the biggest sexual pull from culture?**

**Are you protecting yourself from this pull? How well do you filter out culture?**

This sex-filled culture isn't the only problem you have to deal with. On the other side of the coin is the teaching some Christians push that says dating among young adults should be abandoned all together. Or, they encourage a return to the idea of "courting." Dating should be kept as a family affair with the young couple spending most of their time with each extended family. Or maybe even picking a location where other friends are present at all times. Both sets of parents and the couple's friend's would be involved in the structure and limits of the couple's dating, with the understanding among everyone concerned that the couple is testing their compatibility for marriage.

**From a Christian perspective, list the pros and cons of this kind of dating?**

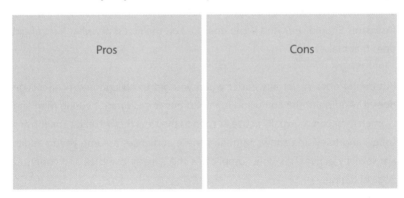

Pros

Cons

**In your opinion, what is the best form of dating?**

Here is the problem: The Bible gives absolutely no direct instructions about the practice of modern dating. In the days of the Bible, marriages were arranged. Fathers would seek sons and daughters to marry who would bring a certain amount of standing to each family. The father of the bride would have to provide a dowry to help the young family get off to a good start in life (as well as compensating the young man for taking the daughter off of her father's hands). Personal happiness was not part of the equation.

Times have changed, some for the better and some for the worse.

So what are you to do? The first thing is to simply acknowledge you're facing a very difficult and complex issue. You have to approach dating very cautiously, especially with the freedom that naturally comes from being a young adult outside of your parent's care. The understanding that guided you as a sophomore in high school won't work as a sophomore in college. You'll need to continue to grow in the knowledge of who you are as an individual and who you are called to be in Christ. As you do this, you'll build confidence in the tempting situations you find yourself in, and in doing so, you'll be more likely to handle each situation appropriately.

**How does one grow in the knowledge of who they are individually and who they are called to be in Christ?**

**How do you respond to sexual temptation in a dating relationship? Why do you think you respond this way?**

## DATING FOR MARRIAGE

How you approach the dating process is more important than you can imagine. There is much at stake. What's learned in the dating process will inform our relationships for the rest of our lives.

As you may know, not all dating experiences are a walk in the park. In fact, you might argue that most of your dating experiences have been bad—and they end even worse. But you can't just give up or pray nothing bad happens. Like I said, there's simply too much at stake.

So how do we prevent these bad experiences? We prevent them by being proactive in the dating process. We lessen the chances that bad things will happen in dating by being sure we understand the purpose of our dating and the goals we have for ourselves while dating. I know, you're reading this and thinking I've just taken all of the romance and fun out of dating. Not so. I'm being honest and upfront about the expectations of dating from a Christian perspective.

From an early age, children begin to form their ideas of masculinity and femininity. By watching their fathers, children will form impressions of how a man lives in the world. They watch how he treats his wife, and they know how he responds to her. They watch him go to work and come home again. From those images and more, a daughter will begin to formulate a picture of the man she'll fall in love with and how she will expect to be treated by him. Dads are the first boy-friends of their daughters. Young men grow up watching their fathers, and when they don't know how else to act, they'll act the way they saw their fathers act.

It's the same with mothers. From birth, their children are watching them, taking note of every conversation and gesture. Daughters learn to become women from their mothers, and sons learn to relate to members of the opposite sex in their experience with their mothers. For most young men, opening the door for their mother is the first time they open a door for a woman. This is why a healthy marriage with a healthy and present father and a healthy and present mother is so important for young men and women. Life's lessons are caught more than they are taught, and there's no more powerful education than watching a husband and wife who love each other interact day in and day out. This is one reason we're dealing with issues of identity and sexuality. Broken homes break more than marriages.

**Was your childhood generally a positive, neutral, or negative experience? Explain your answer.**

**Name three things you've noticed of your actions in your dating experience—negative or positive—that are a result of your relationship with our mom or dad.**

1.

2.

3.

**Who have you looked to in the past for dating advice? Parents? Siblings? Friends? Church leaders? Was it usually good advice or bad advice? Explain your answer.**

Churches also need to be more open in their discussion of dating. There are at least two very bad results from the church's silence. First, by making dating and sexuality off limits, the silence makes the topics more enticing by inadvertently making them more attractive. By making sex something you can't talk about in church, sex then becomes the "forbidden fruit" and the very thing we desire the most.

The second problem is there's no alternative view offered in the cultural discussion of masculinity, femininity, sexuality, love, and relationships in general. With no other vision put before us, we begin to believe the cultural lie that "everyone is doing this" because everyone we see on TV is living this way.

I believe following Jesus is the best way to live. I believe the Scriptural teachings on sex and marriage are some of the most beautiful recorded anywhere.

> **Wives, submit to your own husbands as to the Lord, for the husband is the head of the wife as Christ is the head of the church. He is the Savior of the body. Now as the church submits to Christ, so wives are to submit to their husbands in everything. Husbands, love your wives, just as Christ loved the church and gave Himself for her to make her holy, cleansing her with the washing of water by the word. He did this to present the church to Himself in splendor, without spot or wrinkle or anything like that, but holy and blameless. In the same way, husbands are to love their wives as their own bodies. He who loves his wife loves himself. For no one ever hates his own flesh but provides and cares for it, just as Christ does for the church, since we are members of His body. For this reason a man will leave his father and mother and be joined to his wife, and the two will become one flesh. This mystery is profound, but I am talking about Christ and the church. To sum up, each one of you is to love his wife as himself, and the wife is to respect her husband.**
> *Ephesians 5:22-33*

Paul telling husbands to love their wives as Christ loved the church is an unforgettable image of love. When a wife sees her husband loving her like that, she responds the way the church loves the Lord. The issue of who's in charge, who plays what role, never comes up. Not when the husband and wife are being loved like that.

**How is marriage typically depicted in culture?**

**How is culture's understanding of marriage similar or different to the way we see it described in Scripture?**

| Similar to Scripture | Different from Scripture |
| --- | --- |
|  |  |

Here's the problem. Having a faulty image of marriage will affect how we date. Christ-followers date for a purpose. The ultimate purpose, of course, is to discover the person appropriate for marriage and life together. But there's more to dating than that. In fact, one of the most obvious but overlooked purposes of dating is practice. That's right *practice*.

For some reason, our culture tells us we're to be born as adults when it comes to our relationships, but nothing could be further from the truth. Human beings are helpless when born and clueless when it comes to a relationship with the opposite sex. Dating is where we learn. It's practice.

Dating is also how we can find out if God wants us to marry someone at all. See, not everyone finds love. Marriage isn't for everyone. There are those who are called to live single. The apostle Paul points this out in his letters to the early church. To be single is to be able to live with a singular focus on the work of the kingdom without having to think about family needs. I've seen this for myself. On several occasions, mission needs have opened up at different places around the world. On these occasions, several single people were able to respond faster than anyone. Furniture was put in storage, apartments were subleased, condos or houses rented out, and suddenly they were off to the ends of the earth. The church should learn to appreciate those brothers and sisters who are called to live a single life rather than trying to fix them up with distant relatives.

There's another important point to remember. You and the person you're dating have a future. You are responsible to Jesus for the future of the person you're dating. Christ-followers are stewards with all that Christ entrusts to us, including and most especially, our relationships. Every person we encounter should be better, more like Christ, more useful to Christ, because of their relationship with us. At no time should anyone be less because they have dated a follower of Christ. At no time should they be wounded because they dated a follower of Christ.

**Read the following verses and record how Scripture instructs us to handle our relationships.**

**1 Corinthians 15:58**

**1 Thessalonians 5:11**

**Hebrews 10:25**

**GRAY AREAS**

Now, I'm not naïve. I understand emotions are sometimes fragile things. People get their feelings hurt in dating. Having said that, most of the time people get hurt because of lies, dishonesty, and the varied games we play while we're dating. This is unfortunate and needless. We should be upfront in all of our relationships, especially dating. Remember that dating is practice. You may not meet the love of your life immediately. Therefore it is important to practice well so you're ready for when you do.

## FINDING MR. OR MS. RIGHT

Every relationship is a gift. We don't earn them or deserve them. Christ gives them to us, like everything else in our lives, for our enjoyment and to help us become more like Him. This means every relationship teaches us something. By the time we find the person to whom we get married, we've spent our entire lives building a picture of what "Mr. Right" and "Ms. Right" looks like. We take a little bit from our parents (the images can be either positive or negative), or our favorite movie star and local heroes from our childhoods. We take something we like from that person, something else from another, and one last thing from this one to form a composite picture of the person we're looking for. We place this picture in our minds and then compare everybody we meet to that picture. That's why if and when you finally meet Mr. or Ms. Right, you feel like you've known this person all of your life. In some ways, you have. You've been building a picture of them for most of your life.

Everyone you date adds to this picture. There are some things you liked about the other person. Keep those. There are other things you didn't like. Let go of those. In each dating experience, take a little time to think about what you liked, what you didn't like, and why. Understanding the reasons we respond to certain characteristics provides a unique insight as to how we're thinking about ourselves, others, and relationships in the future.

By the way, when Abraham sent his servant to find a wife for Isaac, the servant prayed God would lead him to the right person for his master. What was his criteria? Kindness. He was looking for a woman who would not only offer water to him, but to water his camels as well. Camels, when thirsty, can drink up to a third of their body weight in water. Watering camels is no small task. Rebecca volunteered to do both.

What strikes me as funny about this is of all the young adults I speak to about the characteristics they're looking for in the person they marry, kindness is never on the list. In fact, saying the word "kindness" will automatically delete someone from the pool of potential mates. Can you imagine the conversation?

"Mike, what's this person like?"

"The best thing I can say," I'll respond, "is to tell you they are one of the kindest people I've ever met."

End of discussion. Interesting, isn't it? One of the first things on God's list isn't even on our list. Seems to me there is something wrong with our expectations.

**What's on your list? Make two lists of essentials and non-essentials that you're looking for in someone to marry.**

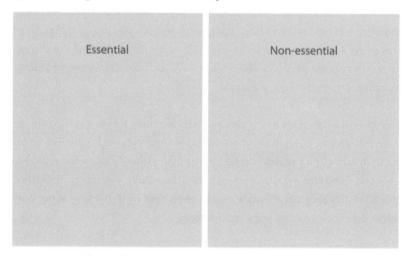

| Essential | Non-essential |
| --- | --- |

Dating also teaches us patience. Most of us can't wait to be in love. We watch the movies and the television shows about the moment when we finally meet our soul mate. Fireworks will explode and there will be music in the air.

Sadly, fireworks only last a few minutes. We have a series of moments where, for an instant, we truly believe the person we're currently dating is the "one." Then, after a few more dates, the very things we once thought were cute now become grating. We seem to fall in and out of love overnight. Not really. What we're feeling isn't true love. Authentic love is tougher than that. So we learn to be a little leery of our initial reactions to first introductions. We learn to walk a little slower, watch a little more carefully. Relationships take time. Patience, as in most things, is a virtue in matters of the heart.

Time is essential to dating. It's all about time. It takes time with another person to see if you're compatible for a lifetime together. It takes time to know the person well enough in the present to understand, or at least not be too surprised as to how that person will react in the future. It takes time to figure out if you can trust this person with your true self. It takes time to find out how deep his character is. Does she just talk? Or does his actions back up his words? These are important things to know. After all, this decision, the person whom you decide to marry, is one of the most important decisions you will ever make.

## SEX OUTSIDE OF MARRIAGE

You have a future. You won't always be in college. You won't always be in your first job. Sooner or later, if God leads you to marriage, you'll realize you love the person you're dating as you have loved no other. You'll start to see yourself spending the rest of your life with this person. In your imagination, you'll see your future, and this person is always in those pictures. Dating is about your future, and you can't ever forget this.

With your future in mind, I want to move to a subject that always comes up when you talk about dating—premarital sex. Most of the time, the question is couched in different terms. The person will want to know "how far can a Christian can go" on a date. The question isn't about geography. Young adults want to know the rules. Is kissing OK? Hugging? What about touching? Holding hands? And then, we start using baseball analogies.

Let's back up a little as we begin to answer this question. First, I want to remind you that God created sex. God gave sex to His children for the physical expression of love and to have children. The love between husbands and wives can be hard to express in words. What we can't express in words, we express in touch—this powerful gift God gives us. Through the gift of sex, a husband and wife can tell each other "I love you as I love no other." In the sanctity and sanctuary of a committed marriage, there is nothing more real or pure than the gift of sex. In the act of sex, souls touch and become one. In a committed marriage, the marriage bond is deepened and the relationship is strengthened.

But outside of a committed marriage, sex can be harmful. As I mentioned, in the act of sex, souls touch, but because there's no relationship, the language of sex has nothing to say and worse, the souls of two people touch and then are pulled apart. The souls tear when they're pulled apart. Over time, the tear will heal, but every healing leaves a scar—scars that have no feeling. In our hook-up culture, countless young adults have numbed their souls to the reality of true love because they have been scarred by past relationships. When authentic love presents itself, the young adult can't feel it.

**Have you been scarred by a previous relationship? Have you dated someone with a scarred past? If so, how did these scars affect the relationships?**

**If you haven't experienced these scars yourself, how have you seen the effects in other relationships?**

**Are you currently in an unhealthy relationship sexually? Whether you are or not, what barriers can you set up now to make sure you remain pure before God?**

The world will tell you it doesn't matter. You're a sexual creature; therefore, sex is natural, and you should enjoy whatever kind of sex you desire whenever you want. Anyone who tries to limit your sexual expression is just dealing with their own hang ups.

But it does matter. You matter. You have a future. There will come a time when you will want to tell someone you love them as you have loved no other. In that moment, you will want to offer your best self. You owe it to the one you will marry. You owe it to yourself.

So, how far can you go? Outside of sexual intercourse I don't know if there's a definite answer. But here's what I do know. We are biologically programmed to want to have children in order to ensure the survival of the human race. In the act of foreplay, our bodies are biologically preparing for sex. If we're not careful, we'll cross a line where biology will take over and our bodies will do what it's designed to do—procreate, not to mention a host of other things we don't want or aren't ready for.

For that reason, it's best that you never put yourself in a situation where you might lose control of your reactions. What that line is for you, only you can know. That's why I want you to keep your dating fun. Learn to be with the other person. Learn what makes her laugh. What makes him tick? Don't rush into sex while you're dating. Sex wasn't designed for dating. Trust me; there'll be plenty of time for it once you're married.

# SESSION 5

*Divorce*

# SMALL-GROUP EXPERIENCE

*Watch the corresponding video from the Teaching DVD, then launch into the discussion guide below.*

**OPEN**

Take turns allowing group members to share two random idiosyncrasies (a peculiar behavior or way of thinking) about themselves—the stranger the better. Consider giving an award for the most peculiar or eccentric trait.

Our mannerisms and habits reveal a lot about us. Likely they're deeply ingrained and almost impossible to change. The same is true of our pasts; we may carry deep wounds, and we certainly can't change what has already taken place.

Many people in and out of the church are affected by divorce, whether directly or indirectly. Let's spend some time discussing why so many relationships end in our culture.

**DISCUSS**

- *What stood out to you from the video?*
- *What was your relationship like with your parents? If they divorced, how did that affect you?*
- *What effects of divorce have you seen in your circle of family and friends?*
- *Why do you think divorce is so commonplace today?*

Read Galatians 5:22-23.

- *Give an example of how your relationships display the fruits of the Spirit.*
- *How are obedience and service essential to a relationship? What happens if one is missing?*
- *In what ways could you improve your respect, honor, and service to others?*
- *How can a couple discern whether their relationship is healthy? (Refer back to Galatians 5 for a cheat sheet.)*

- *What kinds of struggles often lead to divorce? Develop a list of ideas for overcoming each situation you identified.*

Consider spending time with a seasoned married couple this week. Talk with them about the characteristics they find essential in a mate. Discuss their willingness to stay together through life's inevitable ups and downs.

## APPLY

Mike said in the video, "Marriages break, and there's not enough duct tape in the world to put them back together."

- *If you've experienced divorce yourself or with your parents, what fears do you have?*
- *Read Deuteronomy 31:6 and 2 Corinthians 1:8-11. What do these passages say about overcoming fears? How can these verses help you have hope for the future?*
- *What steps can a person take to heal from a divorce?*
- *What role does forgiveness play in that healing? Who might you need to forgive today?*
- *How can you better extend Christian hospitality to others? What things can you do to show love to those hurting from a divorce?*
- *What can you do to ensure strong, godly relationships in your future?*
- *How can a healthy Christian community help you maintain your focus on God's best?*

## PRAY

Close in prayer asking for the ability to develop and maintain strong relationships. Pray that God would allow couples who model biblical dating and marriage for each person to follow. Ask for the wisdom and strength to seek God's best for a possible future marital relationship.

**THROUGH HIS GRACE AND MERCY, HE GIVES US A WAY TO LIV THROUGH OUR FAILURES. FORGIVEN AND A LITTLE WISER, W CAN MOVE ON. OUR GOD IS GREAT ENOUGH TO TAKE THE MESSE OF OUR LIVES AND DO SOMETHING BEAUTIFUL WITH THEM.**

Do you remember how old you were when you first learned that when things break, they can't always be fixed? Maybe it was your favorite toy or your favorite stuffed animal. Something fell off. Something tore or broke, and this time there just wasn't enough Elmer's glue or duct tape to make the needed repair. Sometimes things break—like marriages. And similar to toys, they can't always be fixed. When you were little, you took the broken toy to your parents. You were shocked to realize there was something they couldn't fix. Now, that we're older, we take our broken things to God and we're surprised there isn't some divine magic to simply make everything better.

The hard reality of life is that we live in a broken world. The hard biblical truth we seem to have to relearn every day is that we're broken people. Sometimes when things break, they just can't be put back together. This brings us to our question for today. What happens when a marriage breaks?

I know. We've grown up with all the church platitudes. Marriage is sacred. Marriage is forever. What God has joined together, let no one tear apart. I know, but we live in the real world, and sometimes the real world just doesn't work out that way. All of us have had those dreams about falling in love and living happily ever after. Then, we get married and we find out "ever after" isn't as long as we thought it was. In our world, broken people get married and make broken marriages. It's just a matter of time before the marriage itself breaks. We know that divorce is a reality we live with. In fact, if all the studies are correct, more and more of us are living with the reality of divorce. Maybe your parents have gotten divorced. Maybe a brother or sister got divorced. Maybe your grandparents got divorced, or maybe you did.

**Have you been directly affected by divorce? If yes, how so?**

**When you hear the term *divorce*, what 's the first thing that comes to your mind?**

## JESUS ON DIVORCE

So how does the church respond to divorce? What are we supposed to do, and how do we deal with this growing reality? Does the church have something to say about divorce? Well, yes we do and it begins, as all things must, by seeing what Jesus had to say about the subject.

**Some Pharisees approached [Christ] to test Him. They asked, "Is it lawful for a man to divorce his wife on any grounds?" "Haven't you read," He replied, "that He who created them in the beginning made them male and female," and He also said: "For this reason a man will leave his father and mother and be joined to his wife, and the two will become one flesh? So they are no longer two, but one flesh. Therefore, what God has joined together, man must not separate." "Why then," they asked Him, "did Moses command us to give divorce papers and to send her away?" He told them, "Moses permitted you to divorce your wives because of the hardness of your hearts. But it was not like that from the beginning. And I tell you, whoever divorces his wife, except for sexual immorality, and marries another, commits adultery."**
*Matthew 19:3-9*

In Matthew 19, a group of Pharisees come to Jesus to argue about divorce. You can tell by the tone of the questions and some of the subtle hints in this passage these are not questions seeking knowledge. These religious leaders did not want to talk to Jesus and understand His perspective or gain new insight. This was a trap. The religious leaders wanted to see if Jesus would disagree with Moses who had given them a way to divorce their wives.

Now, you have to understand that divorce in the day of Jesus was a simple matter of paperwork. If the woman was displeasing to the husband (and it could be for any reason), he would simply write her a certificate of divorce and she would be sent out from the family. I'm being a little simplistic in my explanation, but not much. Women had no rights in this process.

In the days before women's rights, it would be very difficult for her to get a job or make a living without going into prostitution or begging. To divorce a woman without ample way for her to be taken care of was just about the same as giving her a death sentence. So you have to understand that Jesus is responding to the needs of unprotected women.

The Pharisees came to Jesus and asked, "Can a man divorce his wife?" It's interesting that they didn't ask if a woman can divorce her husband. That was not even thought of then. But they came to test Jesus to see if, and on what grounds a man could divorce his wife.

Jesus responded, "What does the Scripture say?"

The Pharisees' minds went back to a passage in Deuteronomy where Moses had given them permission to divorce (see Deut. 24:1-4). Jesus, instead, went to the second chapter of Genesis. This goes back to the very first biblical teaching on marriage, blessing the union of Adam and Eve. This was the prototype of all marriages that would ever follow. The concluding line of Genesis 2 says, "This is why a man leaves his father and mother and bonds with his wife, and they become one flesh" (v. 24).

I find it interesting to note the biblical story doesn't emphasize the woman leaving her home. The emphasis is on the man leaving his home. "A man leaves his father and mother." He will need to not be dependent on his parents, but be able to stand on his own, before he is ready for a marriage.

The two will then become one flesh.

**What do you think it means for two to become one flesh?**

The emotional, physical, mental, and spiritual bond between the husband and wife in a good marriage makes them one. This bond is so strong a third entity beyond the husband and wife and the marriage itself is created in the birth of their children. Chris and Craig, my two sons, are a little bit me and a little bit Jeannie. Jeannie and I are one in them.

So Jesus went back to the very beginning and said, "What God has joined together, man must not separate" (Matt. 19:6). If the marriage is of God, then how do people write laws that tear apart things that God has joined together?

Their reply: "Didn't Moses say we could do this?"

Jesus almost interrupted them saying, "Hey, he gave you a way out because of your hardness of heart, because of your disobedience, because you won't listen to what God's trying to tell you, because you just want a way out."

Jesus made the point that divorce is the result of hardness of heart. The strong implication in Jesus' teaching is someone in the marriage isn't obedient to the teaching of God on marriage. Disobedience is the root cause of divorce.

**How has hardness of heart resulted in continued disobedience in your own life? Give examples.**

**Have you see this kind of disobedience within marriages? This could be with marriages in general or marriages that you're directly connected to.**

There are generally two considerations for divorce.

One is adultery. If one of the partners has an affair, then the other partner can make the choice to be released from the marriage (see Matt. 19:9). Sometime in that affair, the marriage died.

The other is abandonment by an unbelieving spouse. If the unbeliever leaves, you aren't obligated to stay in the marriage. The divorce will simply recognize what has really happened—in that the two were no longer one (see 1 Cor. 7:10-16).

We have in our culture everything from a no fault divorce to very complicated legalities where people are advising brides and grooms to negotiate a good pre-nuptial agreement. This is sort of like agreeing on the terms of the divorce before the couple is even married.

Divorce is devastating. It always is. Divorce disrupts the picture of Christ in His relationship with the church. But because we are a sinful people, God has given instructions through the revelation of Scripture to deal with marriages when they have been broken. Like the Pharasees, we must not use these reasons as a way out. The decision to divorce is not ours to make—it's God's. If you have done everything in your power to reconcile the marriage, and God has given you permission to leave, then you may leave. But reconciliation, and the attempt to salvage the marriage commitment should always be the first priority.

These were all issues the early church had to deal with, and it's clearly saturating our culture today as well. So what are we to do?

## PREPARATION FOR MARRIAGE
Let's do what Jesus did and go back to the very beginning. If we are going to engage this divorce culture we live in and do something about the pain this causes, the first thing we have to do is make a covenant with each other that we're going to take marriage a lot more seriously. We're going to restore marriage to its rightful place. We're going to live respecting the holiness of marriage and recognize the sacredness of matrimony.

Now, in political debates, you'll hear a lot of people say, "We believe marriage is sacred. You can't mess with it." But the truth of the matter is that we don't live that way. Here is my proof: A young couple will come to me and say, "Mike, we're going to get married on this date, at this time, at this place. We want you to do the ceremony." The minister is often the last piece added to the picture. By then the couple has already rented the limousine and the tuxes, the bridal gown has been bought, the rehearsal dinner plans have been made, and the honeymoon has been reserved. Then they come to get the input of their pastor.

They ask, "Do we have to do anything for you before you do our wedding? Is there any premarital counseling we'll need to do?" They fully assume we will rubber stamp this process because they have already met the criteria of a happy marriage: they're cute.

They started dating because they were cute. He's cute. She's cute. Together they're cute. Her friends had to check him out and see if he was cute—and if they made a cute couple. Once her friends give her the thumbs up then the dating relationship can continue. If his friends say, "Yeah, she's cute," the dating relationship moves to the next step. By then we want to meet parents. The parents approve by saying, "Hey, you're so cute together. You'll be really happy."

So they're ready for a cute marriage, and they come to the pastor to ask about the ceremony, wanting to see how they can have this marriage of "cute."

Imagine their surprise when I look at the groom and say, "Tell me where you were and what was going on in your life when Jesus gave you permission to take this relationship to the next step." Or I turn to the bride and say, "Tell me where you were when you understood that to follow Christ, the next step of your discipleship was to become this man's wife." "Tell me where you both were when the Lord gave you permission and invited you into this marriage relationship."

You would think I was speaking a foreign language.

"But we're cute."

No, I don't do weddings because they're cute. I do weddings because they are the will of God.

I will have testimony of other believers that this couple believes it's God's will for them to become a family and engage in this holy moment of matrimony. I will have seen evidence in the couple's life that God can work in and through them and bring something significant for His kingdom.

What is at stake in a marriage isn't you or me as husband or wife. It's the lordship of Jesus Christ. Jesus is head of the house. The marriage belongs to Jesus—not to the husband and not to the wife.

**Among your circle of friends, how serious is a marital bond? What about from culture's perspective?**

**Read Ephesians 5:23-30. Why is it important for a Christian marriage, especially one that others are witnessing, to remain committed to the marriage vows? How does this Ephesians passage specifically emphasize this importance?**

One of the things we have to do is restore marriage to its proper place under the lordship of Jesus. I'm not trying to take the romance out of marriage, but I am trying to restore our understanding that Jesus is Lord of all, including marriage. One of the forgotten purposes of marriage is the process of making better disciples of both the husband and wife. The marriage is supposed to bring the couple closer to each other and closer to Christ. Authentic love releases the deepest essence of the husband and the wife. The wife is more of who she's created to be because of how her husband loves her. The husband, in turn, is more of his true self because of the way his wife loves him. The role of steward informs all of our relationships. The wife is the steward of her husband, and the husband is the steward of his wife.

**What does it mean that a husband and wife need to be good stewards of each other?**

**From your understanding, what is the purpose of marriage in the first place?**

**In your own words, define authentic love within the context of marriage.**

On the flip side, inauthentic love within a marriage shrinks the husband and wife and makes them less, not more, as a person. You know relationships like this. And it's easy to tell authentic from inauthentic, isn't it? Authentic marriages are those where the husband and wife love each other in the love of the Lord. They are the ones that create little mini churches in their neighborhood. You remember that house. It was the house on your street where all the kids played. The grass didn't grow. There was always a baseball path worn in the yard, and bicycles in the driveway. The reason was that Ma loved Pa, Pa loved Ma, and they created this little whirlpool. Ma and Pa loved the kids, and the kids got sucked into this whirlpool. If you got close enough, you got sucked into this whirlpool of love, too. And I'll tell you, if a kid can find anything, a kid can find love.

That's the purpose of marriage. It's a husband loving his wife so that people will begin to understand in a real and tangible way what the love of Jesus for His church looks like. It's a wife loving her husband in such a way that people will understand what the love of the church looks like when it's lived out.

## BREAKING POINT

Even with our best plan, sometimes things break, don't they? So how does the church respond?

First, we respond more quickly. Most of the time, the last place you can bring up that things aren't going well is the church. Churches must work to provide safe places for couples to talk about what's going on in their marriages before small cracks rupture into giant canyons. Older couples, those who've been married for 20 or 30 years need to find newlyweds to mentor. Remember, a lot of people who get married have never seen a successful marriage. Having pictures of healthy marriages to relate to and conversations with those men and women who are in these marriages would be one of the best things we could do for our newlywed couples.

**Name three couples whose marriages are how you desire to model your own marriage. Beside each name give a few reasons why you listed them.**

1.


2.


3.



Another aspect of our quick response would be to communicate the fact that struggles are normal in marriages. If these struggles are handled redemptively, these uncomfortable moments can be used as opportunities of growth. Unfortunately, our culture's understanding of marriage is so shallow that most people see a moment's unhappiness as the first sign the marriage is doomed. Churches are going to have to create conversations for couples to be able to handle their challenges in pro-active and growth inducing ways.

Then, as clumsy as this may sound, the church needs to be better at caring for people going through a divorce. Right now, during a divorce, both the husband and the wife drop out of church. Friends are afraid to take sides, unsure how to react to the new realities when their friends' divorce. The husband and wife then either find other churches or drop out of church altogether.

The church, like any army, has to learn to better treat its wounded. Yes, this is not to condone right or wrong, but to simply admit that Jesus is the judge and we're not.

**What other ways can the church rise up to support both those who are experiencing marital problems and those who have gone through or are currently going through a divorce?**

If we take out the "blame pie" of what happened and cut it up where both gets one piece of their responsibility, sure someone would get a bigger piece of the pie, but each would still get a piece. Both are responsible for the health, and sadly, the destruction of a marriage. By no means is only one person to blame, and rarely is there just one victim. It takes two to kill a marriage.

Now, the divorce doesn't happen when the judge signs the papers. The divorce happens when one or both of the marriage partners decides to stop doing what it takes to make the marriage work. And sometimes, when the decision is made there is nothing anyone can do.

But we can pick up the pieces.

And how do we that? We do our best to keep the conversation open between the parties. We counsel those involved about the fairest way to move forward. You might have major problems with what you're reading right now. You might think I'm being soft on divorce. I'm not. I believe God created marriage to last a lifetime. Yet, I have to live in the real world. In the real world, people make mistakes and marriages fall apart. The church has to learn to minimize the damage.

This means working with divorcing spouses so they're able to move on with their lives as best they can. It means helping them experience the forgiveness and healing of Christ, recovering a sense of purpose and meaning. Once the damage is done, no purpose is served by increasing the suffering of the parties. We have to remember that Jesus died on the cross for just such sins as these. Once He has forgiven, no one else dare bring judgment.

**How do you typically think of someone who has been through a divorce? Is this the correct way of thinking? Why or why not?**

## FORGIVENESS AND HEALING

What about those of us who were caught in the crossfire of divorce? What about those of us who don't have a relationship with our mothers or our fathers because of divorce? What about those of us who were pawns in our parents' fighting?

Again, a word of forgiveness is needed. Our parents are human, and sometimes they're more human than we wish they were. Forgiveness is releasing the other person from the expectation that they can fix the wrong they did. They can't. Even if your parents wanted to, they can't undo the pain the divorce brought to you. You have to find a way to deal with the pain yourself. Of course, we do this best through prayer as we seek the healing only Jesus can bring.

**What do each of the following verses say to those experiencing the need for healing?**

**Psalm 55:22**

**Psalm 73:26**

**Matthew 11:28-30**

**2 Corinthians 12:9**

Part of that healing is the invitation to move forward to your own future. Your parents' mistakes aren't your mistakes. Their decisions aren't yours. You're not trapped or held hostage by your parents' decisions. You've been set free in Christ and that means you're free to find your own purpose and joy in Christ.

**Have you learned to move on from past failures of your own or failures of your parents? If yes, how so? If no, what is holding you back from accepting freedom from forgiveness in Christ?**

Getting caught in the crossfire of divorce has wounded many people. Your life may be a mess because of divorce. You may have a father you don't know because of the divorce. You may have a mother you don't understand because of the divorce. You may have had really bad Christmases because of a divorce and really complicated family vacations. You may even say, "I'm never going to get married." But you don't have to bear the pain for somebody else's mistake. Jesus died on the cross once. There's no need for you to do it again.

Sure, the ultimate and divine purpose of marriage is "until death do us part." But we're human, and humans mess up. Our failures need not be fatal. Christ has given us a way through this. First, He has restored the sanctity of marriage. Second, through His Spirit, He gives us the grace to live lovingly in a marriage. Through His grace and mercy, He gives us a way to live through our failures. Forgiven and a little wiser, we can move on. Our God is great enough to take the messes of our lives and do something beautiful with them. He's that good of a God.

Yes, divorce happens, and yes divorce is a failure, but the grace of God means that our failures or the failure of our parents' relationship won't have the last word in our lives. Grace has the last word. It always does.

GRAY AREAS

# SESSION 6
*Sexual Identity*

# SMALL-GROUP EXPERIENCE

*Watch the corresponding video from the Teaching DVD, then launch into the discussion guide below.*

**OPEN**

This session contains some pretty sensitive topics. Take a moment to express the need for confidentiality, respect, and grace during the forthcoming conversation.

- *What stood out to you most from the video?*
- *What questions do you still have?*

**DISCUSS**

- *How do you differentiate between sin and bad habits? Is there a difference? Explain your response.*
- *How would you summarize God's plan for sex and sexuality? Read 1 Thessalonians 4:3-8 for clarity.*
- *What about His plan is most difficult for you?*

Mike explained in the video that our spiritual wiring is connected to our sexual wiring.

- *What connection do you see between purity and growing spiritually?*
- *Why does sexual sin often carry more guilt and shame than other sins?*
- *What kinds of wounds have you seen others experience from acting outside of God's plan?*
- *What are the short- and long-term consequences of those wounds?*
- *Do you find that you try to justify your sins, particularly when it comes to sex? Why or why not?*

Regardless of who you are or what you've done, God loves you. He will forgive you (see Hebrews 4:15; John 7:53–8:11). He wants what is best for you. That means following His plan—even if you've gotten way off track.

## APPLY

- *What steps can you take to overcome and/or avoid temptation?*
- *Read Jeremiah 7:24. What situations or people need to be avoided to help you succeed? How can your small group help?*

Whether or not you personally struggle with sexual issues, many in our society do. We're called to love others, and that includes treating everyone with dignity and respect. Jesus set the example for us, and then He called us to follow Him.

Read Matthew 22:37-38; John 20:21.

- *Why do so many Christians struggle to show grace and love to people who've committed sexual sin, particularly sins related to homosexuality?*
- *How can Christians display God's love to those struggling with sex and sexuality?*
- *What practical things can your small group do to care for the unloved in society?*

## PRAY

Finish up the session with a time of individual reflection and repentance. Then close in prayer, asking for forgiveness, healing, and a renewed strength in the face of temptation.

IF YOU LOVE GOD, THEN YOU LOVE OTHERS. JESUS IS ALWAYS GOING TO BRING YOU PEOPLE WHO NEED TO SEE HIS LOVE IN REAL LIFE.

The baby boomers are coming into retirement age. They are getting a little older and age does things to you. So we invented Viagra. We can't cure the common cold, but that one we figured out. We don't want anybody or anything—even Mother Nature—limiting our sexual freedom. We want to be able to do what we want to do, when we want to do it, and with whom we want to do it. Our goal is to fulfill whatever desire we might have.

**Generally speaking, how have Christians dealt with the changing ideas in our culture about sexuality and sexual practices?**

So as a believer, what does it mean to live under the teaching of Christ in our post-modern culture that just oozes sex and promiscuity? As you would imagine, the Bible has a lot to say about this. You may know some of the passages. In fact, they may be so familiar to you I'm afraid you won't really listen to them. Sometimes we have a tendency to say, "Oh, I've heard that" and click our brains off. But if you do you won't hear the whole story and you'll end up making some easy assumption.

I want to be really sure you hear what I'm teaching. This is a crucial issue in our culture because it impacts so many lives.

## ROMANS ON SEXUALITY

Let's take some time studying the first chapter in Romans.

> I am obligated both to Greeks and barbarians, both to the wise and the foolish. So I am eager to preach the good news to you also who are in Rome. For I am not ashamed of the gospel, because it is God's power for salvation to everyone who believes, first to the Jew, and also to the Greek. For in it God's righteousness is revealed from faith to faith, just as it is written: The righteous will live by faith. For God's wrath is revealed from heaven against all godlessness and unrighteousness of people who by their unrighteousness suppress the truth, since what can be known about God is evident among them, because God has shown it to them. ... Therefore God delivered them over in the cravings of their hearts to sexual impurity, so that their bodies were degraded among themselves. They exchanged the truth of God for a lie, and worshiped and served something created instead of the Creator, who is praised forever. Amen. This is why God delivered them over to degrading passions. For even their females exchanged natural sexual relations for unnatural ones. The males in the same way also left

natural relations with females and were inflamed
in their lust for one another. Males committed
shameless acts with males and received in their own
persons the appropriate penalty of their error. And
because they did not think it worthwhile to acknowledge God, God delivered them over to a worthless
mind to do what is morally wrong. They are filled
with all unrighteousness, evil, greed, and wickedness. They are full of envy, murder, quarrels, deceit,
and malice. They are gossips, slanderers, God-haters,
arrogant, proud, boastful, inventors of evil, dis-
obedient to parents, undiscerning, untrustworthy,
unloving, and unmerciful. Although they know full
well God's just sentence—that those who practice
such things deserve to die—they not only do them,
but even applaud others who practice them.

*Romans 1:14-32*

Anytime we talk about sexuality and proper sexual behavior, somebody in the room will point to Romans 1. They'll open up the Bible—and it's usually a big Bible. They'll point and say, "This is what God says, right here. It's in God's Word."

Yes, it is. But you have to understand what Paul is doing in Romans 1, especially when you get to the passages where he lists all the sins. Now, understand Paul, more than being a theologian, more than being a writer, is the pastor of a church. As pastor of a church, he loves to preach. He especially loves to preach where nobody has preached before. He even says in the letter to the Romans that it frustrates him to go to a place where somebody else has already preached Jesus. He doesn't like to go and build on another man's foundation. He loves to be the first one there.

Here's the background. At the writing of this letter, Paul had never been to the church in Rome, but he's writing to give them his travel plan. He's saying, "Here's what I want to do. I want to come to Rome. I want to preach and teach while I'm in Rome, and I want you to get to know me and hear my message. I want you then to support my missionary work on into Gaul (which is the Roman provinces that make up modern-day Spain and France). I love missionary work, and I want to go and preach where nobody has ever preached Jesus before. That's why I'm writing you this letter: to tell you I'm coming and to introduce you to myself and to my message of the gospel."

Paul tells them he's going back to Jerusalem to deliver the gift for the saints. He has taken up a collection among the Gentile churches because the church in Jerusalem is starving to death. There has been a famine in Jerusalem. There are Christians who can't find work, so they're hungry. Paul sees this as an opportunity to express Christian brotherhood to both Jews and Gentiles.

Now, let's get back to Romans.

Paul begins writing this letter. In Romans 1:16-17, he says, "I have an obligation to preach to everybody . . . Gentile, Jew . . . everybody. I want everybody to hear the good news of Jesus Christ, because I believe the gospel is the good news of God for salvation. And here's why I have to preach it." Then we have the list describing our fallen state in verse 18 and following. If we don't believe in the fall, then we just aren't paying attention. He lists a lot of sins in here. So we read selectively and will pick out a couple of sins—the handful that don't apply to us—and condemn them. The guys who are like me? They're going to get mercy. The guys who commit those sins? They're going to receive God's wrath.

**Have you ever done this? What kind of sins are you quick to condemn while ignoring your own?**

**When you see sin in other's lives, is your initial response one of love or of condemnation? Why?**

Let's continue with a key moment in chapter one. It comes at verse 17 when Paul writes, "For in it God's righteousness is revealed from faith to faith, just as it is written: The righteous will live by faith." The just man—the righteous man—will live by faith, with everything focused on the lordship of Jesus Christ and the future of His coming kingdom.

If you're like most Christians, you've probably gone through the list in Romans, thinking, *that's me, that's me, this one's me, NOT me, this one's bad*. Now remember, Paul has never been to Rome. He is introducing the gospel to the Roman church. He describes the fallenness of humanity and he ends with the ultimate wickedness. And not only do they continue to do wrong, but they celebrate the people who do wrong. Evildoers become the heroes of the culture.

Isn't this similar to the culture we live in today? Evildoers become the people we celebrate in our books and our movies—those people who break the rules and get away with it. These people flaunt the rules, break the rules, and get away with it. They become heroes—outlaws—in our culture and we celebrate them. Paul is saying, "Our world is so upside down that we literally cannot tell right from wrong. So when somebody is losing we celebrate like they're winning. And when somebody is winning we despise them as if they're losing.

**Where do you see this most often in culture?**

**Why do you think this happens?**

Pay attention to the way Romans 1 works. First is the denial of God, of God's existence, His authority, His reality, His law, and His purposes. "I'm not even sure there is a God," I can hear them say. But Paul tells them, "You know there is God. He made Himself known in all kinds of ways. You just didn't want to see. Because if you recognize there's a God, that means you will have to change." That's why a lot of people you talk to who claim to have intellectual problems with Christianity actually have moral problems with Christianity. If Jesus is Lord, they have to change the way they live and they'd rather hang on to their lives than declare Jesus is Lord. So they play word games with Jesus and still continue to live the way they want.

## SEXUALITY AND SPIRITUALITY

Let's break this down. In the Ten Commandments we learn that God is the only Person—capital P—with the gravitas, the weight to hold your life in its proper orbit. If you put anything or anyone in the center of your life, your life flies out of orbit. It can't hold. It doesn't have the gravity to do it. So when God isn't in the center of someone's life, the first place it shows up is in sexual confusion. Hang with me here as I explain.

**What are your thoughts on the previous statement? Why is sexuality the first thing to break down when God isn't at the center of our lives?**

It's interesting that marital problems are usually first discovered when the sexual relationship between the husband and wife goes awry. The first place troubles will show up—if they're angry with each other, lying to each other, or one of them is backing out of the relationship—is in the bedroom.

Why? Sex is the most fragile and the most sacred part of the marriage. It's the most honest part of the marriage. So, if you ever have to go to marriage counseling, one of the first things a good marriage counselor will ask is "How are things in the bedroom?" Sex is the heart indicator about how things are in a marriage. When things get out of whack in your relationship with God, the first place it shows up is in sexual confusion.

Have you ever noticed how many songwriters, poets, and artists refer to sex in spiritual tones? They'll stress the spiritual nature of sex. And they're right. Your sexuality is deeply connected to your spirituality. It's the language God gave between a man and a woman to express your deepest self in ways that words cannot. When God isn't the center of your life this is the first place it shows up. It shows up in sexual confusion of promiscuous sex. It shows up in the sexual confusion of a gay or lesbian lifestyle. That's what Paul is saying.

This is as far as a lot of you read. Paul goes on to list a lot more who will not enter the kingdom of God. The church has just picked this one.

Do not hear me making light of sin or sexual confusion. Do not hear me making more of it, either. We pick this one. We don't ever read the rest of them. When I was growing up we did the same thing. The pastor would sweat and get all red in the face, and really bear down on this. This is just one part of sin. It's the part when desires become your God, and what you feel and what you desire becomes the way you make your decisions.

Paul addresses this in another letter, 1 Corinthians 6. Now, I know some of you are thinking, *Man, this is a new day and we've got to have a new way of thinking, because the Bible doesn't understand anything we're going through.* Then you need to read the Bible. That would be my suggestion to you.

Paul has a problem church in Corinth. As a pastor he felt like he was the father of all these churches, and every parent has a child who needs some special attention. Corinth needed that special attention. In fact, they needed so much special attention that Paul gives warning in his letter to them.

I'm not writing this to shame you, but to warn you as
my dear children. For you can have 10,000 instruc-
tors in Christ, but you can't have many fathers. For
I became your father in Christ Jesus through the
gospel. Therefore I urge you to imitate me. ... I will
come to you soon, if the Lord wills, and I will know not
the talk but the power of those who are inflated with
pride. For the kingdom of God is not a matter of talk
but of power. What do you want? Should I come to
you with a rod, or in love and a spirit of gentleness?
*1 Corinthians 4:14-21*

Now if you're a father, you understand Paul's mind-set here. Paul is referring
to an issue in the early church where the Corinthians were saying, "We love
Jesus. Jesus loves us. Our spirits are saved. Our bodies can do whatever they
want to do."

**Do you know anyone who thinks this way? Do you or have you ever
thought this way? Why do you think our minds sometimes shift to this
poor way of understanding God's grace?**

Paul says to go back and think about their bodies. Their bodies were created in
the image of God. Their bodies were part of what God gave them. And somehow
the bodies themselves reveal the very nature and presence of God. For instance,
if they enter into relationships with a prostitute, because Christ is inside of them,
they have taken Christ to that prostitute. Paul says that's not the way to live.

Here's what Paul says in 1 Corinthians 6:

> **Run from sexual immorality! "Every sin a person can commit is outside the body." On the contrary, the person who is sexually immoral sins against his own body. Don't you know that your body is a sanctuary of the Holy Spirit who is in you, whom you have from God? You are not your own, for you were bought at a price. Therefore glorify God in your body.**
> *1 Corinthians 6:18-20*

Now, again, we live in a culture that says, "Wait a minute. I don't want anybody to limit my freedom. I don't want anybody telling me I can't do something." But when you realize Jesus Christ paid for you with His death on the cross, you'll come to Him and respond the only way you can by giving your life back to Him. We come to Him, Paul says, as slaves. We give up our future. We give up our decisions. We give up our dreams. We give it all to Christ, and we live to serve Him. All of our decisions have to be made under His direction and with His permission. Any decision not made that way is sin. Anything not from faith is sin. Paul is saying, "Listen, your body is owned by the Lord Jesus Christ. You are not your own. Therefore, glorify God in your body." Your body points people to the reality of the risen Christ. The decisions you make with your body are not yours to make. The decisions I make with my body are not mine to make. We are under His lordship.

**Paul says that your body, sexuality, decisions, choices, desires, and everything are not owned by you but by God. How does this make you feel?**

**What areas in your life are you least likely to release over to God?**

We don't like being controlled like that, do we? We don't like being owned by anything. We don't like anybody telling us we can't do something because it would be harmful to us. We want to be free, but freedom in Christianity was never license to sin. Freedom in Christ means the ability to respond to His calling and commands without hesitation.

## OUR AIM

In regards to our sexuality, Paul gives us a good goal in Ephesians.

"Husbands, love your wives." Did you notice the command? Love your wife—not protect her, not take care of her. No, "love your wife." Now, if he had put a period there we'd all feel warm and fuzzy. We'd go cross stitch it and put it on our refrigerator. But he doesn't. He continues: "just as Christ loved the church and gave Himself for her" (Eph. 5:25).

"As Christ loved the church"—Christ died for the church. He laid His life down for the church. He pursued the church. He took care of the church. He did all of that.

The presence of a Christian marriage makes known the presence of the living Christ Himself. It becomes a sanctuary and a tabernacle where Christ is worshiped and people are brought to know Him. Your marriage, my marriage, is a sanctuary—a church—where people come to know Christ.

> **This mystery is profound, but I am talking about Christ and the church. To sum up, each one of you is to love his wife as himself, and the wife is to respect her husband.**
> *Ephesians 5:32-33*

Let's go back to what was lost in the garden of Eden. Remember, Paul talks about this in Romans 1. What happened when Adam and Eve turned away from God? It's as if the world began to break and fall apart. So how in the world do we get back to where we were and what was lost? We do it through the resurrection of Jesus Christ and in a relationship with Him. The key relationship now is no longer between the husband and wife. The key relationship is now between the husband and Christ and the wife and Christ.

Paul also embraced single living. Why? Because Jesus did not marry. Paul also tells the early church it's better for some people to remain single so that they can respond to the calling of God immediately. They will be able to respond to God as He leads.

## HOMOSEXUALITY

By now you might be upset with me because I haven't yet discussed the issue of homosexuality. But in order to rightly understand this type of sexuality, we had to first examine a proper relationship—one designed by God.

**Have you put thought into the issue of homosexuality? If so, how do you view this issue?**

We have a growing awareness of gays, of lesbians, their needs, their lifestyles, and their choices. Several in this community are being very demanding about what they want from culture. Let me stop right here and say that the church has blown this one. We have messed this one up so bad, because we've come across as hating. If you've heard that message from the church for any reason, I want you to know, more than anything—and I don't care where you are, who you are, where you've been, what you're into—Jesus loves you.

**Do you typically respond to those who live a homosexual lifestyle out of love, out of hate, or do you ignore them altogether? What makes you respond this way?**

Now, hear me. We're never given permission to judge another human being. Why? Because we don't ever have the whole story. We don't ever have all the facts.

Judging isn't my job. My job is an evangelist, a preacher. My job is to tell everybody the good news that Jesus died for them and Jesus now lives for them, and there is a future for them. There's a hope for you, and there's a life for you if you take it from Him.

The bottom line is, I'm Mike Glenn reading and interpreting Scripture and doing the best I can. And from what I've seen in Scripture, homosexuality is just not God's best for you. The reason it bothers Him is that it hurts you. That's what He's concerned about.

If you struggle with homosexuality and if we could talk, you would likely tell me, "I was born this way." My answer to you is that we live in a fallen world where people are not born perfect. And our sin has brought on desires that are not pleasing to God. But even our desires are under the lordship of Jesus Christ. I have temptations. I don't want them, but they're what attracts my attention. They can grab hold of my attention, and they're what I think about if I'm not careful. And same-sex attraction may be your temptation.

But hear this: Temptation isn't sin. It's the opportunity to sin, but it's not sin. If temptation is sin, then Jesus messed up. Because I have this longing, because I have this desire, because I have this opportunity, that's just temptation. That's not the sin.

**Name one or two things that you have always struggled with. Why do you think these are so difficult for you?**

**How often does the temptation of these things lead to sin?**

Here's another question many people ask: can I act out on same-sex attraction and still be a Christian? Probably so. Just like there are drug addicts who are Christian. There are many people who have other issues and are still Christian. So if this is where you are, and if this is what you're dealing with, it's just yours to deal with.

Now, I understand that sometimes people point and say, "Hey, this sin is worse than that sin is."

No it's not. Some of us will be judged harsher by God because we slept around, or got a divorce, or have a gambling problem—and the damage done is worse than the people who are dealing with same-sex attraction.

We can't rank sins. We can't rank these issues. Everybody's dealing with one, and they're just as devastating to one life as any other sin is to another.

So what do you do?

First, I want to talk to you as a Christian with a gay friend. Maybe you're straight and you don't understand. Let me tell you something. If you love God, then you love others. Jesus is always going to bring you people who need to see His love in real life. They will say, "The church has rejected me. Christ has rejected me. See how they have treated me." You could be the person who rejected them. But then again, you may be a friend—possibly one of their only friends. You don't have to agree with everything they say or do. I don't agree with all my friends about everything. But you have to be their friend.

You may uptight and say, "What will people think if they see me hanging around people like that?" They'll think you're a lot like Jesus. You don't have a right to dismiss anybody from the love of God, nor judge anyone.

Show them God's love anyway.

**Are you currently showing those who are different from you the love of Christ? If not, with whom will you start?**


**How would people you're different from describe you?**


If you're dealing with homosexuality in your own life, it's just where you are. It's yours to deal with. Now again, I don't want to underplay it, but I don't want to overplay it either. God has desires for you. You live in a broken world where things get turned upside down. But the good news of Christ is yes, He died for us. The great news of Christ is that He lives for us. And He will come to you— inside of you—and change what you want. He'll change your dreams, change your hopes to align with His hopes and His dreams. That's part of what we call sanctification: the continuing process of salvation.

If you are dealing with homosexuality, here's what I want to say to you: it's not God's best for you. I don't want you walking away from this study angry or hurt. I really don't. I'm very aware of the pain that this issue brings up. I'm very frightened that what I've written would wound anybody. I don't want to do that.

I'm a guy who is just like you in more ways than you would want me to be. I'm not smarter; I'm just older. You may say I have wisdom, but I also have scars.

Some that know me might say what a great husband I am. But if Jeannie were listening she would say that's a new phenomenon. I was a lousy husband for a lot of years, but I learned. I've made a lot of mistakes—things I would be so ashamed of if you found out. I would be so embarrassed if they ever became public. I'm not a judge. I'm not the jury. I'm just one guy who found that in a relationship with Jesus Christ things could change in my life—and they can change in yours too. That's my testimony. That's my life. What was broken, He has fixed. What was wounded, He has healed. My old desires—the things I wanted that I knew were not good for me—He took away. I don't want those things anymore. It didn't happen overnight, but through a lot of prayer, Scripture reading, and conversations with older brothers and sisters in Christ.

That's what I want for you. I want you to find God's best for you, too.

**Briefly describe what this looks like in your life right now. What's God's best for you in your current situation?**

Christ's agenda is His love for you. That's it. You're important to Jesus. If you had been the only one to fall, Jesus would have still gone to the cross. Do you know that? Had you been the only one to mess up, Jesus would have died for your sins.

Now He will take you where He finds you, but He won't leave you there. In the Bible we have all these stories of Jesus welcoming friends—broken, blind, lame, and sin-covered—"losers" of all kinds. Jesus would stop and talk to them. He would ask their names. We're told that Jesus had to go a particular way so that He would be at a place called Jericho and Zacchaeus could be found (see Luke 19). Jesus went another particular way so that He would be at a well in Samaria where a woman could be found (see John 4). Through these stories, we come to realize that Jesus seeks us out where we are, and then He leads us to where we need to be.

**Do you ever think that because of sin you're too far removed for God to meet you where you are? Are you there now? Why is it dangerous to think this way?**

We were born into a broken world—a broken world that too often breaks us. If that's where you are, tell Him about it now. You won't tell Him anything He doesn't already know. You're not going to shock Him, so just be honest.

*Jesus, this is where I am.*

*This is what's going on.*

*This is what I can't get out of my head.*

*This is what I can't figure out. Help me, Lord.*

GRAY AREAS

# SESSION 7

## *Living in the Land of Shadows*

# SMALL-GROUP EXPERIENCE

*Watch the corresponding video from the Teaching DVD,
then launch into the discussion guide below.*

**OPEN**

Go around the room and finish the following sentences:

*The best job I ever had was …*

*If I could do anything for a living, it would be …*

*One reason I'm here today is …*

**DISCUSS**

• *How do you respond to Mike's explanation that we don't live in a Christian nation?*

• *What challenges do you see for Christians today?*

• *How do those challenges hinder your ability to see God's work in your life? In the world?*

• *What did you learn from the stories of Daniel and Joseph?*

• *Why do you think God allows believers to experience hardships and persecutions?*

• *Read Titus 2:11-14. What perspective does this passage give on the adversity we face?*

In the video Mike said, "Jesus has restored meaning to our work."

• *What does this mean to you in your current life stage?*

• *How has your perspective of work changed throughout the years?*

• *Would you rather be an important person or do important work? Which is more valuable? What would culture say? Why?*

• *What can you do to move in the right direction?*

• *What things can you do to be missionally-minded wherever you are?*

• *What's the riskiest thing you've ever done for Christ? How did God work in that situation?*

**GRAY AREAS**

**APPLY**

Read John 15:19; 17:14-19.

> - *How can you follow Jesus' teaching in these verses? What does this look like on a daily basis?*
> - *What kinds of things should Christians do to be better witnesses? What should we avoid doing?*
> - *What does it mean that you have been sent into the world (see John 17:18)?*
> - *How does that change your perspective on work? Relationships? Money? Time? Trials?*
> - *Of everything you've learned in this study, what has challenged you the most? Why?*
> - *What gray areas need more clarification? Identify a trusted source (person, book, Bible passage, etc.) to help you study further.*

**PRAY**

Lead in a time of prayer based on your study this week. Thank Jesus for His work on the cross and for the hope we have in His return. Thank God for giving us strength to endure through difficult times. Pray that the group would continue to grow spiritually and follow Christ no matter the cost.

**DO NOT BE CONFORMED TO THIS AGE, BUT BE TRANSFORMED BY THE RENEWING OF YOUR MIND, SO THAT YOU MAY DISCERN WHAT IS THE GOOD, PLEASING, AND PERFECT WILL OF GOD.** Romans 12:2

We do not live in a Christian nation. Do you understand that? If not, read it again. We do not live in a Christian nation.

Perhaps the United States was founded as a Christian nation, or maybe even on Judeo-Christian principles. I will leave that up to historians to debate. Here's the point I want to make, and it's not debatable: You and I, as believers in 21st century North America, do not live in a Christian nation. Nothing in our nation's popular culture or our society's prevailing mind-set supports our faith. Our culture doesn't encourage the Christian faith (or any faith at all). We live in a nation that is, at best, neutral to faith. And in growing sectors of our society, there is a growing hostility to the Christian faith.

**Have you seen hostility toward the Christian faith? If so, how?**

**Why do you think our culture, once heavily influenced by Christian faith and principles, has steadily shifted over time to become a culture of hostility toward Christians?**

As you might imagine, there have been intense and varied reactions to the growing acceptance of this reality. Some Christian leaders have advocated the election of Christian politicians so our perceived Judeo-Christian heritage could be protected. Others have wanted to withdraw totally into Christian communities where Christian schools and Christian businesses allow us to only engage with other Christians. As other minorities have done, the thinking goes, Christians should cluster together and have a Christian sector in major cities across America. And cultures throughout history have responded this way with varying degrees of success.

Here's why I'm making such a big effort to try to understand this reality that we don't live in a Christian nation: Until this clicks—until we grab hold of this new way of thinking—we'll keep trying to live by the wrong map. See, most of us have a map of reality in our heads. This map is made up of the assumptions we have about how the world works and how we live in it. If our mental maps don't match the reality we live in, we're constantly frustrated.

Let me give you an example.

I grew up in Alabama, and as you would imagine, I have a very good map of Alabama in my car. The problem with having a very good map of Alabama is this: I live in Tennessee. A very good map of Alabama is worthless when I'm trying to drive through Tennessee. If I'm going to arrive at my desired destination, I need to change my map. In the same way, most of us need to change our map of reality if we're going to successfully live in post-Christian America. Until we do, we're going to be constantly frustrated and ultimately defeated.

To my brothers and sisters in Christ: relax. Take a deep breath. We've been here before. Remember, we're not the first believers to live in a situation where a government and/or ruler didn't support our relationship with God. We're not the first people to live in a time or place that's hostile to our faith. Not only have we been here before, but we've had pioneers of faith who've actually thrived in situations just like ours. There is much these people can teach us about how to respond to living faithfully in our 21st century, post-Christian American culture.

## WHAT DANIEL TEACHES US

First, there's Daniel. Do you remember the story? Daniel and his friends are taken from Jerusalem to the capital of Babylon because they were chosen by the Babylonians as young men having desirable skills and abilities. They were brought to the capital to be trained to serve as counselors in the royal court. When Daniel and his friends arrive, they are taken to the king's palace and served food from the king's table. Now, this food was not kosher. That is, it wasn't prepared in keeping with Jewish law. From the way it was described, the food wasn't really healthy either. And Daniel recognized this wasn't good for him.

Daniel refuses to eat the food the king sent him. He explains this to the guard who is over them and says, "I can't eat this. Let me have a vegetarian diet." Now this guard would pay for any mistake with his life, so he was very reluctant to let Daniel try this experiment. But he was willing to do it within limits, so he gave Daniel a period of several days. At the end of those days, Daniel and his friends looked better and performed better than everybody else. So the guard in charge changed everybody's diet.

Because Daniel was faithful to the Lord's teaching about food, God granted him and his friends favor. They were found to be 10 times better in all areas of education and learning. They were better in Babylonian literature. They were better in finance and in accounting—everything! As the story develops you know that Daniel becomes one of the most trusted advisors to a series of kings.

**How have you seen God's favor because of your obedience to Him?**

**Is God's favor contingent on whether or not we are obedient? Why or why not?**

What, then, should we learn from Daniel's story?

The first lesson Daniel will teach Christians living in 21st century America is that we have to take control of what goes into our minds and into our bodies. Obviously, we need to learn to maintain better nutrition. We live in a culture that celebrates fast, fatty, high sugar, processed foods. These foods are now known for the damage they do to our health. Diabetes is climbing at unprecedented rates. Certain cancers are being traced to our dietary habits. Strokes are traced back to our high intake of salt and result in high blood pressure. The list goes on and on because we don't discipline ourselves to eat in a healthy manner.

Many believers have had trouble maintaining healthy habits. We either ignore it or we pay too much attention to it. But God gave us each a brain, a heart, and a body to get us there. Our bodies have to be in shape and prepared so that we can put our love in action for the people we need to love. We need healthy bodies to serve. We need to control what comes into our bodies and start living a healthier lifestyle.

We also have to control what comes into our minds. The messages of our culture aren't conducive to a Christ-follower's life. These come in all forms of media, not just what we see on television. Negative messages are in our magazines, in the content of our video games, and in the movies we watch. By the time students leave high school, they'll have witnessed several thousand murders and many more thousand acts of violence on television. Seeing this kind of violence on television numbs the minds and hearts of all who watch it to the reality of death and suffering in the lives of the people around us.

What makes our image-driven culture so dangerous is what these images do in our minds.

We don't just watch television. Television imprints images on our minds. We don't just listen to the radio. These words get inside our heads and begin to form our worldview—that is, the way we see things around us, the way we see values and truth, the way we understand how we are to live in the world around us.

All of this comes to us through the culture. This means we, as responsible Christians, have to learn to control and take responsibility of what comes into our eyes, ears, and minds. I know. You might say to me, "Mike, I can't control what I think." Yes you can. It takes a little practice, but you can do it.

How do you practice this? First of all, stay in the Scripture. "Be transformed," Paul writes, "by the renewing of your mind" (Rom. 12:2). Stay part of an accountability group. Journal and keep your thoughts honest. This is what Daniel did.

**What else helps you prepare your mind for pure and Christ-focused thoughts?**

**Read the following two verses and comment on how each addresses protecting your thoughts against the lure of culture.**

**John 15:19**

**2 Corinthians 5:17**

Controlling our thoughts, however, doesn't mean withdrawing from culture. Daniel teaches us that as people of faith we should be the exact opposite of culture. Now that's a tough tightrope to walk, but it's the commandment we have. Daniel and his friends proved to be 10 times better at the things the Babylonian king needed them to do. God granted them wisdom so that they would be elevated to a platform where they could give witness and glory to God as they do on several occasions in the stories that follow.

In the same way, the post-modern church is meant to be 10 times better than the world at what the world does. We have to be 10 times better attorneys. We have to be 10 times better accountants. We have to be 10 times better CEOs. We have to be 10 times better computer programmers.

**Are you driven like this? What area in life are you not giving God your absolute best—your "10 times better"?**

**How do you typically view your work? How do you decide how much effort you're going to put into your work? (School work, paid work, unpaid work, etc.)**

In the fall we lost meaning in work. God told Adam,

> **The ground is cursed because of you. You will eat from
> it by means of painful labor all the days of your life.
> It will produce thorns and thistles for you, and you
> will eat the plants of the field.**
> *Genesis 3:17-18*

So we go to work—we slave 8 hours, 10 hours, 12 hours a day. We come home. We're exhausted. We're brain dead. And yet we often don't know if we've done anything meaningful.

But Jesus restores meaning for us. Paul tells us, "Whatever you do, do it enthusiastically, as something done for the Lord and not for men" (Col. 3:23). Whatever your job, you do that job like you are doing it for Jesus. It may be a very important job or a menial job, but you do that job as if Jesus were your employer. You do that job to the very best of your ability, bringing excellence to everything you do, because your very work is an act of worship.

**Have you ever thought of your work being a form of worship to God Himself? Do you agree with this? Why or why not?**

When I was growing up, the maintenance supervisor of my little church was a man named Mr. Green. He worked part time at the church and also at the mill across the street from the church. I had never seen a church building this spotless. The floors were always shiny. There was never any dirt. It was an immaculate facility. And if you asked Mr. Green why he cleaned the church like he did, he would say, "Jesus will be here Sunday." He had taken the lowly job of cleaning the church—waxing floors, cleaning up after messy teenagers in a Sunday School room, and cleaning the bathrooms—and made his work a very act of worship. So when the Lord came to be with His people on Sunday the building would be ready for the presence of Jesus. Mr. Green understood that whatever his hands found to do, he was going to do it as to the Lord (see Eph. 6:7).

## WHAT JOSEPH TEACHES US

Joseph is the second person I want to bring to your attention. You likely know his story. Joseph was sold into slavery by his brothers. He had been wrongly accused of a crime. He had been falsely imprisoned and then forgotten. Later, when there was a crisis in the nation, Joseph was remembered and brought to Pharaoh. Joseph interpreted Pharaoh's dream and proved to be an invaluable counselor to Pharaoh and his leadership. Joseph was honored not only in Egypt but in Israel as well.

Let's examine two interesting points from Joseph's story. The first is obedience. What if Joseph had given in to despair while he waited for God to remember him? Now, remember how many times Joseph had been betrayed and wronged. His brothers beat him up, threw him in a hole, and then sold him to slavers. He was bought as a slave, falsely accused of a crime, forgotten in prison. On any number of those occasions he could have given in to the despair and said it doesn't matter—even surrendering his relationship with God. But then when God had come for Joseph, he wouldn't have been ready to serve.

**Have you ever been tempted to give in to despair because of surrounding circumstances? If yes, explain what happened.**

Too many times we get into a situation and think it doesn't matter. We think it's too late. If God were going to do something He would have done it by now. So we give in to the despair and we sacrifice our righteousness. Then the moment comes and we're not ready. When the moment came for Joseph, he was ready. He stepped in front of Pharaoh and interpreted his dreams. God gave Joseph the interpretation because of his intimate relationship with God.

If we are going to survive in post-Christian America it will be because Christians—the church—take on a new understanding of holiness. It means being totally committed to, and always focusing on, our relationship with Jesus Christ—so we don't disqualify ourselves for those moments when Jesus wants to use us.

Are you ready to be used by God? List three things that need to change in your life so God can more effectively use you for His kingdom purposes.

1.

2.

3.

The second part of Joseph's story I find interesting is the theme of forgiveness. Before Joseph's life the response to being wronged was "An eye for and eye and a tooth for a tooth" (see Ex. 21:24). Joseph was the first one to choose not to seek revenge. Look at what he does in Genesis 50.

> When Joseph's brothers saw that their father was dead, they said to one another, "If Joseph is holding a grudge against us, he will certainly repay us for all the suffering we caused him." So they sent this message to Joseph, "Before he died your father gave a command: 'Say this to Joseph: Please forgive your brothers' transgression and their sin—the suffering they caused you.' Therefore, please forgive the transgression of the servants of the God of your father." Joseph wept when their message came to him. Then his brothers also came to him, bowed down before him, and said, "We are your slaves!" But Joseph said to them, "Don't be afraid. Am I in the place of God? You planned evil against me; God planned it for good to bring about the present result—the survival of many people. Therefore don't be afraid. I will take care of you and your little ones." And he comforted them and spoke kindly to them.
> *Genesis 50:15-21*

Joseph's brothers had wronged him, but he forgave them, saying, "What you meant for evil, God meant for good."

**How easy is it for you to forgive those who have wronged you? Is there someone who still hasn't seen your love through forgiveness?**

The third part of Joseph's story I find interesting is that it was Joseph who interpreted Pharaoh's dreams. Our culture is filled with dreams—with people who want to see their lives differently, who want to see something significant happen. The reality is that no one gets up in the morning and says, "Today I'm going to wreck my life beyond all recognition." No one has decided, "This is the day I'm going to make stupid decision after stupid decision and totally destroy my life and my family."

One of the things Christians need to do is to be in the position to help our culture understand that yes, it's a good thing to want loving relationships, but here's how God says you can do it. Yes, it's a good thing to want to be successful, but here's how God defines success. This is one of the things Joseph teaches us.

**How can we be engaged in the conversations of our culture so that we're in a position to help them define their dreams?**

In Hebrews 12:4, there is a blunt reminder: "In struggling against sin, you have not yet resisted to the point of shedding your blood." In other words, the writer of Hebrews tells the early church, and those of us since then, "Stop whining." The fact of the matter is, there are people around the world who are suffering much more than we are. So one of the things I want to say to the 21st century church in post-Christian America is stop whining.

I hear all the time where people say the Supreme Court threw God out of school. I want to see the man who is big enough to throw God anywhere! This is the same God who went into Egypt and pulled His people out of slavery into freedom. This is the same God who went into the fiery furnace and brought Shadrach, Meschach, and Abednego through it. This is the same God who stayed all night with Daniel in the middle of the lion's den. This is the same God who went into that garden tomb on that first Easter morning and pulled His Son back from death.

And now you tell me the Supreme Court has a ruling and God can't go into a public school. If you're serving a God who can't get into a public school because the Supreme Court said He couldn't go there, you're serving the wrong God.

You may not know this, but while in Babylon, the people of Jerusalem faced a particular crisis. They believed God actually lived in the temple. It was His house and when they went to worship they would go to the temple. They had a sacred space where they would worship. In Babylon all that was destroyed, the temple was gone and they were in a new country. You hear this in Psalm 137: "How can we sing the LORD's song on foreign soil?" (v. 4).

The interesting thing that happened while they were in the Babylonian captivity was the development of the synagogue. The men of the community would gather around and study the Word. Historians believe a lot of the Bible we have now was written down and copied during the Babylonian captivity. Until then it had been mostly an oral tradition. But the Babylonian captivity forced people to write things down, and they became students of the Word.

**Are you a student of the Word? Do you crave it? What practices can you establish for yourself so you can more consistently read and study God's Word?**

## SURVIVING IN A POST-CHRISTIAN 21ST CENTURY AMERICA

To survive in post-Christian 21st century America, the church is going to have to return to the centrality of the Word. It will require people understanding what Jesus is saying and how His Word is to be applied. It will be people reaffirming our identity again and again by studying and learning the Word.

We also need to be engaged in every area of culture. That is, we need to have Christian artists—people who are writing the great novels, writing the great songs, and performing the great music. We need leading thinkers in every area of conversation who are Christians. We cannot retreat. We cannot give up. No army yet has won any war by retreating.

When you're faithful to this, in due time the Lord will lift you up. He has promised that. He's not putting you in a place or a platform for self-gratification—but one where you can bless the name of Christ, bless the community, and give witness to His glory.

**How are you currently engaging culture with the good news of Christ?**

**What's one truth you learned from this study that will guide you to engage culture differently than you ever have before?**

There are four areas where the church has traditionally engaged the culture: Medicine, Poverty, Education, and Evangelism.

- With medicine, we were the first ones who took care of the victims of the plague in the Middle Ages.

- With poverty, we saw Mother Teresa gain credibility when she ministered to the lepers in India. One of the things the gospel does is restore dignity to the person. Poverty breaks dignity down. By working with a person, helping him understand essential life skills, and providing a job and job training, a person is restored to dignity. Traditionally, the church has done very well in dealing with issues of poverty.

- With education, we are reminded that most of the leading universities in this nation were founded by Christians. We need to return to the public forum of education.

- With evangelism, we have shared that the gospel is changing lives through the death of Jesus on the cross. But we live in a time now when the ministry comes before the message—when no one will listen to you until they understand you have something significant to bring to them. So they have to see it before they'll listen to what you say.

**If you were to give the church a grade (1-10) based on how well they're engaging the culture through medicine, poverty, education, and evangelism, what grade would you give? Give a brief reason for your grade.**

|  | Grade | Reasoning |
|---|---|---|
| **Medicine** |  |  |
| **Poverty** |  |  |
| **Education** |  |  |
| **Evangelism** |  |  |

If you come into a community and provide a health clinic, people will want to know what you're doing. You'll have an opportunity to tell them, "This is what Jesus tells us to do." People will listen to you. The ministry comes before the message, and the strange thing is, we've been doing the very same thing on the mission field for years. Now, our own nation is the mission field. So what we have done in Rio de Janeiro, what we've done in countries in Africa, what we've done in Asia, we'll now have to do in the cities of our own nation.

Know this: It isn't a bad time to be alive. This is going to be an exciting time for the church and for our Lord. This isn't the first time we've been here, and God has given us grace to triumph through it all. Seize the moment in confidence. Victory is ours. Our Lord reigns.

# Threads

An advocate of churches and people like you, Threads provides Bible studies and events designed to:

**cultivate community** We need people we can call when the tire's flat or when we get the promotion. And it's those people—the day-in-day-out people—who we want to walk through life with and learn about God from.

**provide depth** Kiddie pools are for kids. We're looking to dive in, head first, to all the hard-to-talk-about topics, tough questions, and thought-provoking Scriptures. We think this is a good thing, because we're in process. We're becoming. And who we're becoming isn't shallow.

**lift up responsibility** We are committed to being responsible—doing the right things like recycling and volunteering. And we're also trying to grow in our understanding of what it means to share the gospel, serve the poor, love our neighbors, tithe, and make wise choices about our time, money, and relationships.

**encourage connection** We're looking for connection with our church, our community, with somebody who's willing to walk along side us and give us a little advice here and there. We'd like opportunities to pour our lives out for others because we're willing to do that walk-along-side thing for someone else, too. We have a lot to learn from people older and younger than us. From the body of Christ.

We're glad you picked up this study. Please come by and visit us at *threadsmedia.com*.

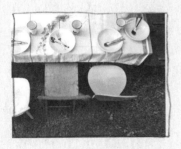